Cunard-White Star
Liners of the 1930s

CUNARD-WHITE STAR LINERS OF THE 1930S

WILLIAM H. MILLER

AMBERLEY

First published 2015

Amberley Publishing
The Hill, Stroud
Gloucestershire, GL5 4EP
www.amberley-books.com

British Library Cataloguing in Publication Data.
A catalogue record for this book is available from the British Library.

ISBN 978 1 4456 4968 9 (print)
ISBN 978 1 4456 4969 6 (ebook)

Typesetting and origination by Amberley Publishing
Printed in Great Britain

Trans-Atlantic passage: the mighty *Majestic* departs from New York's Chelsea Piers in the fading light of a winter's afternoon. (Author's Collection)

CONTENTS

FOREWORD

I met Bill Miller aboard the *Queen Mary 2* during a summer crossing from Southampton to New York. It was a great voyage. Because of his fascinating and interesting talks on the great liners, especially the great Cunard liners, it was also a voyage down memory lane. No company still in the passenger ship business today has the history that belongs to Cunard. It is rich, historic and includes so many great ships. I was enchanted and enriched – and very grateful to Bill, and to Cunard for creating the *Queen Mary 2* to continue the tradition of Atlantic crossings.

Myself, I have a long history with Cunard. My grandfather was with them, then as Cunard-White Star of course, and served in the 1930s in the *Majestic*, *Olympic*, *Laurentic* and *Georgic*. After the Second World War, my father joined the company and sailed as a bedroom steward aboard the *Media*, *Caronia*, *Queen Mary* and *Saxonia*. His sister and my aunt did a stint as a stewardess aboard both *Queens*, the incomparable *Mary* and *Elizabeth*. Coming from Liverpool myself, I served in the late 1950s and early '60s in the *Britannic*, *Parthia*, *Ivernia*, *Carinthia* and *Sylvania*. They were each wonderful ships, of course, and each part of a different age.

I talked about those great times and ships with Bill as we had afternoon tea together in the splendor of the *Queen Mary 2*'s Queens Room. It was true ocean liner style, so much like those good old days on those earlier ships. But now, firmly ashore, I am delighted to write this foreword for Bill's latest book on the Cunard-White Star liners of the 1930s.

Peter Waddington
Lancashire, England
Spring 2015

ACKNOWLEDGEMENTS

As with all books, it takes many hands to compile and complete a project such as this. As author and coordinator, I am most grateful to all. First and foremost, my thanks to Amberley Publishing for suggesting and then following through with this project – and especially to Louis Archard and his fine team. Added special thanks to Stephen Card for providing his superb artwork for the covers and to Peter Waddington for his evocative foreword. Special thanks also to Richard Faber, Michael Gallagher, Michael Hadgis, Norman Knebel and Anthony La Forgia.

Added acknowledgement to Ernest Arroyo, the late Frank Braynard, the late Frank Cronican, the late Harley Crossley, the late Alex Duncan, the late F. W. Hawks, Pine Hodges, Philip King, John Lee, Campbell and Jeanette McCutcheon, Richard K. Morse, the late Charles Swanson, Don Stoltenberg, the late Everett Viez, Steffan Weirauch, Richard Weiss and Albert Wilhelmi. Companies, organisations and societies that assisted include Cunard Line, the Halifax Maritime Museum, National Geographic Society, Steamship Historical Society of America, World Ocean & Cruise Liner Society and the World Ship Society.

INTRODUCTION

The early 1930s could not have been worse for shipping. The North Atlantic had grown very short of its most precious commodity: passengers. The Depression was being felt worldwide. Passenger ships began to sail half-full, and sometimes even emptier, and, with costs cut by their owners, were sometimes scarred in streaks of rust. Future prospects were bleak, of course – the lay-up of ships and the lay-off of crews. The worst scenarios were the complete collapse and bankruptcy of their owners. Cunard as well as its nearest rival, the British-flag White Star Line – owned by the American J. P. Morgan interests until the mid-1920s – were hard hit. Both firms soon found that they had too many ships against far too few occupied passenger berths. One million passengers had crossed in 1930; this dropped by half, to 500,000, in 1935.

Another pressing problem, however, was that both firms were running their top-of-the-line express services with aging, increasingly less competitive super liners. The beloved, four-funnel *Mauretania*, for example, was twenty-three years old by 1930. Company directors as well as the British Government itself were rightfully worried. Comparatively, continental European firms were making important strides. The French had just added the decoratively stunning, art deco-inspired *Ile de France* and planned three more Atlantic liners including the ultra-luxurious *Normandie*; the Germans were adding two mighty greyhounds, the *Bremen* and *Europa*; and even those 'distant Italians' had twin superships in the works, the *Rex* and *Conte di Savoia*. Britain needed to create some retaliation.

By contrast, White Star Line never quite recovered from the tragic loss of the *Titanic* in 1912 and the cloud of the sinking in wartime of their biggest liner ever, the *Britannic*, in 1916. The late Everett Viez, a New York City travel agent and ocean liner enthusiast beginning from the late 1920s, once told me, 'The White Star Line in the twenties was never quite the same. It was not quite as crisp, was even tarnished, and no longer had its high reputation equal to Cunard. There was a certain "first cousin" status about the White Star Line and its ships.'

Despite slowly increasing financial woes, however, White Star Line ordered its biggest liner yet, the 60,000-ton *Oceanic*, in June 1928. A motor ship with three squat funnels, she was intended to break records, being the very first liner to exceed 1,000 feet in length, and altogether would cost a hefty £3.5 million ($14.5 million). Simultaneously, and not to be out done,

Cunard designers planned an even bigger ship, a projected 75,000-tonner (actually in excess of 81,000 tons when completed), which became the illustrious *Queen Mary*. Inevitably, the two British superliners would have been teamed in Southampton–Cherbourg–New York service.

But the *Oceanic* was never to be. Within thirteen months of construction starting at Belfast, the increasingly fragile White Star Line was forced to cancel the order and the small steel skeleton was cut up. But all was not lost. White Star had also ordered, and from same Belfast builders, a more moderate, 27,000-ton 'cabin liner' as they were called, the *Britannic*. The *Oceanic*'s cancellation was later altered to a near-sister, another 'cabin liner', the *Georgic*. That ship would in fact be the very last White Star ship of any kind. By the end of 1930, a full year after the Wall Street Crash, White Star posted losses of £400,000 ($1.9 million). For a company that began passenger service in 1871, even worse times were ahead. By December 1931, its passenger lists had dropped to a scant 250,000.

Both Cunard and especially White Star needed help. The British Government was called upon to assist and, as a result, the House of Commons passed the North Atlantic Shipping Act in 1933. It authorised a loan of £9.5 million pounds ($46.1 million) to Cunard and White Star, divided as £3 million to complete the *Queen Mary* (then enduring a two-and-a-half year delay on the Clyde), £5 million toward building a running-mate (the *Queen Elizabeth*, due in 1940) and £1.5 million working capital. It was all given provided the two companies, once fierce competitors, sensibly merged. And so, on 1 January 1934, Cunard-White Star Limited was formed. It was a name kept in use until 1950 and whose last ship, the *Britannic*, was in service and bore its funnel colours until 1960.

In this marriage of onetime rivals, Cunard – with fifteen liners of its own – acquired ten passenger ships from White Star. These included the world's largest liner, the 56,500-ton *Majestic*. But as the Depression lingered over the Atlantic, like vast storm clouds, the Atlantic passenger trade showed little improvement. The order of the day was rapid disposal and most of them from White Star.

This book has been created – in Cunard's 175th year – as a nostalgic review of those twenty-five Cunard-White Star liners.

Bill Miller
New Jersey USA
Summer 2015

1. MAURETANIA (1907)

In the summer of 1983, I did one of those 'all of Britain' coach tours – beginning in London, reaching westwards to Devon and then north to the Lake District and Scotland, and finally back to London along the east coast. One of our stops was charming Bristol. We had a late afternoon arrival and, quickly after a light dinner, I headed off to a special destination: the Mauretania pub. It was one of the reflective places of wood panels taken just before demolition from one of the greatest and grandest liners of all, the *Mauretania* of 1907. I saw the woods, felt that connection to a ship I'd never seen but knew much about, and also was fascinated by the neon sign outside: it was four grouped Cunard funnels in red and black. What a link!

Cunard built three superliners before the First World War, but lost one, the *Lusitania*, in 1915. After the war, Cunard acquired another superliner from Germany, the *Berengaria*. The *Mauretania, Aquitania* and *Berengaria* were Cunard's post-war 'Big Three'.

The *Lusitania* and *Mauretania* had been, in a sense, the gift of the British Government to Cunard to ensure that the company remained an independent national shipping line in the face of the creation of American tycoon J. P. Morgan's vast international shipping cartel, the IMM, the International Mercantile Marine. He had an ambitious scheme that might have succeeded. Owning the White Star Line, it might have meant acquisition of Cunard as well.

As a result of the encouragement offered by the British Government came two of the finest liners ever built. Some say, from several standpoints, that the *Mauretania* was the most beautiful, most successful and perhaps greatest passenger ship of her time. Certainly, she was a favourite of legions of travellers. She held the trans-Atlantic speed record longer than any other ship. She gave heroic service as a troopship in the First World War and later, painted white, she was used extensively and quite successfully as a cruise ship near the end of her days. There is little doubt that the *Lusitania* would have done as well had she not been tragically sunk by a German U-boat on 7 May 1915 with the loss of 1,198 lives.

For design and styling and even decoration, the *Mauretania* and her near-sister were just about maritime perfection. Alone, the decision by Cunard architects to have the four funnels evenly spaced was brilliant.

Ideas of grouping them in pairs, like the big German liners of the time, were fortunately dropped. With a mast fore and aft, they had great integrity in design, especially when seen from a distance. They were classic ocean liner beauties that maritime historians and aficionados look back upon in cherished nostalgia. This is, of course, an area of great debate. There are those that feel the *Aquitania* was the greater ship, the more beautiful, even the more successful.

While the *Lusitania* was constructed by John Brown & Company on the Clyde up in Scotland, the 31,938 grt *Mauretania* was simultaneously built at Newcastle by another famed, equally accomplished shipbuilder: Swan, Hunter & Wigham Richardson Ltd. She was, rather expectedly, statistically impressive: 790 feet from stem to stern, 88 feet wide and with steam turbines linked to four screws that produced a service speed of 25 knots. Her Blue Riband speed record, set in 1907, was 23.69 knots (and later, in 1909, 25.89 knots). Her accommodations ranged from gilded luxury to bare-steel simplicity for a total of 2,335 passengers in all – 560 First Class, 475 Second Class and 1,300 Third Class.

Like figures atop a wedding cake, the *Mauretania* stood at the very top of a group of liners aptly dubbed 'the floating palaces'. Her interiors represented the very best design and decoration not only from Britain, but from Europe as well. The woods used, for example, were selected from British and French forests. The carving was done to exacting detail. Decoration ranged from French Renaissance to English country. Certainly, the liner's First Class main lounge, capped by a large domed skylight and featuring a marble fireplace at the far end, was among her finest rooms.

First and even Second Class public rooms aboard the *Mauretania* were actually quite modern for their time. They were much less ornate than, say, the big German or even the French liners with all their carved cherubs, busty goddesses, armoured knights and bacchanalian figures. While impractical aboard a ship, fireplaces were considered the height of decorative design. Usually, they were entirely artificial. Passengers sat around electrically lit logs. Also, great glass domes were usually in the centre of a liner, where they could be protected from the fiercest of seas. During the First World War, when the *Mauretania* was trooping, much of her fine wood and glossy marble was covered. When the ship was scrapped in Scotland in 1934/35, it was found that many shafts onboard had been filled with shavings, old rags, and odd bits and pieces used to reduce vibration and rattling. They were also all highly flammable. The fact that the *Mauretania* never had any serious fires is a tribute to her care and her fire watch system.

Another First Class standout was the dining room, a two-deck affair with tables on both levels. A descriptive brochure makes for rather interesting reading: 'When the ship is in evening dress, the dining room is as gay and brilliant as Armenonville in Paris's famous Bois, as socially correct as the Berkeley in London, as impressive for its notables as the Ambassador or the Ritz in New York. It offers a menu which is as cosmopolitan as the people who chatter around the tables.'

In the dining room, the captain's table was placed in the centre. There were expansive arrangements of palms and long-stemmed greens. The very centre section under the glass dome was kept free, however, and used for dancing during the long sessions of dinner. One brochure noted, 'Dining in the *Mauretania* thus becomes, more than ever, a sparkling affair.'

The bigger, more luxurious liners of the day each had a verandah café, a sort of shipboard garden room. Onboard the *Mauretania*, it was all wicker chairs and matching tables and a very contemporary touch: a linoleum floor. There were potted plants, more of those oversized palms and ferns, and hanging flowers.

By 1930, the *Mauretania* was not only the oldest of Cunard's 'Big Three', she was also sailing with too few Atlantic passengers in those early Depression years. Her future was as a cruise ship, offering discount cruises sailing off on escapist voyages and for suitably low fares. Repainted in all-white (which reduced the onboard temperatures by as much as ten degrees in those pre-air conditioned times), she now made few crossings, but instead sailed to the sun-filled tropics. She travelled – and at much slower speed – to places like Nassau, Havana, Port au Prince and Kingston. New types of passengers were recruited. The *Mauretania* even made overnight 'booze cruises', priced from $10 and which offered 14 hours of luxury and pleasure. Appealing to secretaries, school teachers, policemen and civil servants, these sailings departed from Cunard's West 14th Street terminal at 5 p.m., passed out to sea and beyond the 3 mile limit (which meant bars could be legally opened in otherwise Prohibition-era America) and return the following morning at 7. Passengers were often so attracted to the attributes of shipboard life that they graduated to two nights, then three nights to Halifax, five nights to Bermuda, even seven nights to Havana.

In early 1930s newspaper and magazine advertisements, Cunard mounted special promotions for its cruises:

> Cunard Line again does the unusual. The world-famous *Mauretania* in all its splendor and distinction … now at your service for West Indies cruises. A travel opportunity of unprecedented value. Spend Thanksgiving Day in Havana … via the *Mauretania*. She sails from New York on November 19th [1933], stopping first at Bermuda and Nassau. 10 happy, glorious days – and what value for your money! Inclusive rates as low as $140!

By 1934, in the wake of struggling revenues in the lingering Depression and the merger with White Star (creating a combined fleet of no less than twenty-five passenger ships), the older, less economic liners had to go. The twenty-seven-year-old *Mauretania* was among them. Following her last round of summer cruises, she left New York on 26 September 1934 (the same day that the *Queen Mary* was launched in Scotland) on her final crossing to Southampton. She was laid up for a time, but by the following spring, shipbreakers had made an acceptable bid. Great loyalists felt that this grand old ship should be saved, preserved as part of Britain's maritime heritage, of course, but that would have taken lots of money. And quite simply, there was very little money about and especially not money for sentimental museum projects. Before leaving the Southampton Docks, however, there was an auction. Fittings from the *Mauretania* – chairs, sofas, tables, mantelpieces and even wood panelling – were sold to the highest bidders. In the end, the *Mauretania* was finished off at Rosyth in Scotland.

Above: Maritime majesty: the *Mauretania* was one of the most successful, popular and beloved ocean liners of all time. (Cunard)

Left: A section of the First Class dining room aboard the 2,335-passenger *Mauretania*. (Author's Collection)

Above: Atlantic luxury: the First Class palm court aboard 31,938 grt *Mauretania*. (Author's Collection)

Right: Ocean liner amenity: for First Class comfort, the lift aboard the 790-foot-long *Mauretania*. (Author's Collection)

Above: The uppermost deck aboard the *Mauretania* – and with three of her four funnels showing. (Author's Collection)

Left: Departure for Southampton: the *Mauretania* prepares to depart from New York's Pier 54 in this view dated 1932. (Author's Collection)

Above: The late Harley Crossley's painting of the Ocean Dock at Southampton – the *Mauretania* is on the right, the *Olympic* on the left. (Harley Crossley Collection)

Right: Averaging an impressive 25 knots in service speed, the *Mauretania* did six days between New York, Cherbourg and Southampton. (Author's Collection)

MAURETANIA

MAURETANIA
TO EGYPT AND THE
MEDITERRANEAN

CUNARD LINE

PLAN AND RATES

MAURETANIA TO EGYPT
AND THE MEDITERRANEAN
FEBRUARY 16, 1929

Above: Repainted in all-white, Cunard referred to the restyled *Mauretania* as being 'all dolled up'.

Right: Cruising to the historic and sunny Mediterranean in the 1920s. (Norman Knebel Collection)

Opposite: Large, often very colourful booklets that included deck plans, full itineraries and passage rates were produced for long, luxurious, often expensive cruises. (Norman Knebel Collection)

2. BERENGARIA (1913)

Up until the 1960s, Lower Broadway at the bottom end of Manhattan was one of my favourite haunts. The great shipping offices were clustered there and were welcome stopping points to collect brochures, postcards, sometimes those large roll-up posters. I returned home, almost deliriously pleased with my takings. I'd ride that returning Hoboken ferry several times, perched on a wood bench on deck, and passed the time just reading each and every brochure – the sailing schedules, cruise booklets, deck plans and even the fare books. What great fun! The likes of the SS *United States* or even the *Queen Mary* herself might slip past, but I hardly noticed – those brochures were a visual treat.

One of my favourite stops on those maritime expeditions was the great and grand Cunard building at 25 Broadway. It was baronial, majestic, imposing, part maritime museum. In the inner vestibule were the great, high-detailed scale models, made by the Bassett Lowke company, of the *Queen Mary* and *Queen Elizabeth* facing the *Majestic*, *Mauretania* (in her cruising white guise of the early 1930s) and one of the sisters *Caronia/Carmania* (1905). What a collection! I stood and stared and studied – and remained altogether quite mesmerised. In the inner hall, the great booking office with its agents seated at mahogany desks, green lamps and leather sofas, were less visible but well lighted models of the second *Mauretania*, the all-green *Caronia*, the twin-funnel freighter *Alsatia*, and Cunard's very first ship, the little paddle-steamer *Britannia*. But once I decided to leave by the rear entrance, from the door facing onto Greenwich Street. Almost tucked away, in the far smaller, darker vestibule, was yet another great model: the *Berengaria*. It was like discovering buried treasure. A favourite ship of mine done as a huge, detailed model! (Fifty years later, at the splendid Liverpool Maritime Museum, I saw another model of the *Berengaria*, but this one obviously remade from her earlier life as the German *Imperator*. Even if repainted in Cunard colours, the funnels were thinner, as they were in the ship's Hamburg America Line days.)

When this ship first began Cunard service, she was called RMS *Imperator*. Her nationality changed slowly. Cleverly, they recognised her fine qualities and made the renamed *Berengaria* the 'in' ship of the twenties. One traveller, fortunately a millionaire, so loved the *Berengaria* that he booked the same suite aboard her for the next ten years. It was also said that even only the 'very best' dogs sailed in the *Berengaria*. Among them was Hollywood's Rin-Tin-Tin.

The 52,226 grt *Berengaria*, one of the most celebrated North Atlantic liners of the twenties and thirties, had two noteworthy distinctions. She was not built for Cunard nor was she named for a Roman province. In May 1912, she had been launched at the Bremer Vulkan shipyard in Hamburg as the *Imperator* by the German Kaiser, Wilhelm II. Then she was the largest and finest member of the ever-expanding Hamburg America Line fleet (with over 400 ships by 1914). She was also the world's largest ship of any kind – dubbed 'the colossus' of the Atlantic. When she set off on her maiden crossing from Hamburg to New York in the spring of 1913, her statistics were nothing short of amazing: 4,594 total passengers, eighty-three lifeboats, a 90-ton rudder and a columned, two-deck-high indoor swimming pool known as the Pompeian Bath that was larger than the very similar pool at London's Royal Automobile Club.

The 919-foot-long *Imperator* was also the first of three successively larger liners that were intended to place imperial Germany in the forefront of international shipping. The second ship, at over 54,000 tons and 950 feet in length, was the *Vaterland* while the third, the *Bismarck*, would be 56,000 tons and 956 feet in length. Cunard's largest liner at the time was the 45,000-ton *Aquitania* and for White Star it was the 48,000-ton *Britannic*. The tragedy of the First World War and Germany's defeat changed all this, however. The *Imperator* went eventually to Cunard as compensation for the loss of the *Lusitania*; the *Vaterland* hoisted the red, white and blue of America and became the *Leviathan*; and the *Bismarck* joined White Star and became their *Majestic*, replacing the sunken *Britannic*.

At first, this ship sailed as the USS *Imperator*, carrying American troops home from war. Afterward, the 23-knot, quadruple-screw ship was chartered to Cunard for post-war austerity service in 1919/20. Later, she formally joined Cunard, had a thorough refit and, in April 1921, became the *Berengaria*, being named after the wife of Richard the Lionheart (and not the customary Roman province names). She started Cunard's revived and revised express service from Southampton (rather than Liverpool). She was not only the largest Cunarder at the time, but, and despite her German heritage, the Cunard flagship. She was very popular from the very start and, by passengers and crew alike, was dubbed 'the Berry'.

Cunard's express run was offered for all of the year. Summer crossings were often tranquil and sometimes blessed with warm, sunny weather; sailings at other times could be inclement – dark grey skies, heavy rains, strong winds and, in winter, ferociously rough seas and even blizzards could be the forecast. The *Berengaria* was tossed about on several occasions while the *Majestic* was once slammed by a huge wave. The *Aquitania* was once three days late arriving in Southampton after an especially rough crossing and the *Mauretania* was kept at her New York berth at West 14th Street until an Atlantic hurricane subsided.

Counting Hollywood stars, American millionaires and even the very popular Prince of Wales among her passengers, the *Berengaria* had accommodation for a maximum of 2,723 passengers – 972 First Class, 630 Second Class, 606 Third Class and 515 Tourist Class. At Southampton, there were organised tours of legendary ships like the *Berengaria*. Special excursion trains left London's Waterloo station and, for as little as £1 ($4.85 at the time), the British public, who might never travel in such grand ships, had the chance to visit them. They were given walkabouts of the splendid public rooms, viewing suites and staterooms, and might even be given afternoon tea in the ship's restaurant. These visits created memorable occasions.

The *Berengaria* was the only three-stacker of Cunard's 'Big Three'. Those funnels gave her a slight resemblance to the later *Queen Mary*. Because of stability problems in her German days, these funnels had been reduced in height by 9 feet. In addition, tons of cement had been laid in her bottom, heavy marbles removed from her interiors and many ponderous pieces of furniture taken from the First Class quarters. Those stability problems were never quite resolved, however. Cunard added more cement in the early 1920s.

Like all others, even the *Berengaria* carried far fewer passengers on her Atlantic crossings of the early 1930s, the start of the international Depression. On one voyage in 1933, she departed from New York with as few as 300 passengers onboard. Cunard was forced to seek new markets to fill their ships. New passengers were sought and, even if temporarily escaping from the bleak times at home, many of these people had never sailed before. Cheap cruising was the window. The *Berengaria* – soon dubbed the 'Bargain-area' by those remembering her glory days – was sent off on bargain cruises. On 11 February 1932, she sailed off from New York's Pier 54 for a quick, four-day escape to Bermuda. Fares began at $50. There were sports on deck (including passenger boxing matches), a masquerade party, dancing in the ballroom and four-course dinners in the main restaurant.

Like the *Aquitania*, the *Berengaria* was paired with the brand-new *Queen Mary* beginning in 1936. Expectedly, the splendidly gleaming *Mary* had the greater popularity; both the *Aquitania* and *Berengaria* were, as Everett Viez called them in the late 1930s, 'faded English roses'. The plan was to keep the *Berengaria* (and *Aquitania*) in service until 1940, when the new *Queen Elizabeth* was due.

Plans changed, however. The *Berengaria* began to suffer from an infirmity that often affected older liners: fire. Most were caused by worn out, outmoded wiring, often behind wood panels. In 1936, there was a more serious blaze while she was berthed at Southampton's Ocean Dock. Two years later, problems for the *Berengaria* were compounded. She had a very serious fire while lying at New York's Pier 90. US Coast Guard authorities, concerned about the ship's ability to carry American passengers safely, abruptly revoked her sailing permit. Embarrassingly for Cunard, she had to return to Southampton empty and without passengers. Cunard protested, saying the ship was still safe, but then was proven wrong when yet another blaze erupted at Southampton. Indeed, her fate was sealed. She was sold for scrapping in October 1938, and was largely dismantled at Jarrow. Final demolition was not completed for another eight years, however, when her double bottom was towed off to Rosyth and finished off.

Above: German ancestry: when commissioned as the Hamburg America Line's 52,117 grt *Imperator* in 1913, the future Cunard *Berengaria* ranked as the largest ship of any kind in the world. (Cunard)

Right: Between Atlantic crossings, the 919-foot-long *Berengaria* waits at Southampton. (Cunard)

R.M.S. *Berengaria*

Above: A brochure cover from the 1920s – the artist sketch of the mighty *Berengaria* compares her to an earlier, smaller Cunarder. (Norman Knebel Collection)

Right: Baronial splendor: the First Class smoking room aboard the very popular *Berengaria*. (Norman Knebel Collection)

Above: Sea-going luxury: it might be a fine London hotel, but instead it is the palm court aboard the *Berengaria*. (Norman Knebel Collection)

Right: Added amenities: Cunard referred to the *Berengaria*'s indoor pool as the Pompeian swimming bath. (Norman Knebel Collection)

Above: The *Berengaria* berthed at New York's Pier 54 with, among others, the *Scythia*, *Minnetonka*, *Homeric* and *Celtic* in port as well. (Author's Collection)

Right: United nations: in March 1937, five large liners were berthed together along Luxury Liner Row – Germany's *Europa*, Italy's *Rex*, the French *Normandie* and Britain's *Georgic* and *Berengaria*. (Author's Collection)

Above: An aft deck boxing competition aboard the *Berengaria* during a short four-night cruise in 1931. (Everett Viez Collection)

Right: Farewell: the *Berengaria* passes through the Narrows and leaves New York for the last time in 1938. (Author's Collection)

3. AQUITANIA (1914)

Housed in modern quarters at Southampton, the current-day Cunard marketing and sales departments often capitalise on special dates and occasions in the company's history. Public relations and company history experts Eric Flounders and Michael Gallagher are usually responsible and often unearth even the smallest historic details. In May 2014, the 2010-built *Queen Elizabeth* made a cruise around the British Isles that included an overnight stop at Liverpool purposely to celebrate the 100th anniversary of the maiden departure of a most beloved ship, the *Aquitania*.

Ferry across the Mersey! This is among the greatest ports for shipping history – and among the friendliest cities anywhere. On a sunny spring morning, the *Queen Elizabeth* had a glorious reception complete with tooting horns, spraying fireboats and crowded ferries – and this was followed by a visit to another superb collection at the local maritime museum (several different models had been brought out of storage since my last visit here six years ago and there was a special exhibition of ocean liner posters being held). The day was exact: it was exactly the 100th anniversary of the maiden departure from here, from the Princes Landing Stage (now a cruise terminal and pedestrian promenade), of the grand

old *Aquitania*. Thoughtfully, Commodore Christopher Rynd pointed out the wood planking that remains from the *Aquitania*'s berth a century ago.

Grand tribute! Cunard has created some of the finest and most important liners of all time. Just after the turn of the last century, in 1907, the company commissioned two of its finest ships – the big and very powerful near-sisters *Lusitania* and *Mauretania*. But like all trans-Atlantic firms, Cunard, too, needed a third big liner to maintain a weekly 'express service' between Liverpool (later Southampton) and New York. It took seven years, however, to add a suitable running mate. This third ship, named *Aquitania*, was larger still and more elaborate in design and decoration (but not more powerful). Commissioned in the spring of 1914, on the eve of the hugely disruptive First World War, the handsome lines of her 901-foot-long exterior were matched by the high beauty of her interiors. The 45,000-tonner was soon dubbed 'The Ship Beautiful'. To many, she had some of the finest public rooms on all the seas: the Carolean smoking room, Palladian lounge, Louis XVI restaurant and Jacobean grill room. Her indoor pool was decorated with replicas of ancient Egyptian ornaments. And Cunard certainly got their money's worth out of her – she was immensely popular, served heroically in two world wars and completed nearly thirty-six years of service. Rightfully, Cunard planned that thirteen-night cruise around Britain with the theme of the 100th anniversary of the great and grand *Aquitania*.

The *Aquitania* was also a very valiant and heroic ship. Together with the far larger *Queen Mary* and *Queen Elizabeth*, the *Aquitania* – which could carry up to 10,000 troops during the Second World War – was said, by none other than Winston Churchill, to have helped end the war by at least a year.

The *Aquitania* was indeed very special. Onboard, evening celebrations began with a cocktail party (Cunard brass, the Lord Mayor of Liverpool, journalists and TV people), then a gala dinner in the Verandah Grill (with a very well done commemorative menu spiced with lots of photos of the *Aquitania*) and finally (at 10.30 p.m.) blazing fireworks in the middle of the Mersey. At dinner, we were seated next to the manager of the Cunard Building in Liverpool (itself very Edwardian and which is now being converted to a 'cruise centre' that will include a restaurant to be called the Aquitania Grill and which, when reopened within the next few months, is also to include a Cunard museum). Another tablemate was the young creator of a huge website devoted to another beloved Cunard liner, the *QE2*. Myself, I did several TV spots, including one for a Cunard film. Of course, there was also lots of talk about next year (2015) when Cunard celebrates its 175th and when the three *Queens* would be in Liverpool at the same time (late May) and when, on 4 July, the *Queen Mary 2* recreates the very first Cunard crossing (1840) with a sailing from Liverpool to Halifax, Boston and New York. Altogether, a great day, another spirited occasion for Cunard!

As mentioned, Cunard's weekly express service, with a sailing in each direction every week from Liverpool (and later Southampton) and from New York, required a trio of large, fast liners. The company already had

a most successful pair, the *Lusitania* and *Mauretania*, but by 1910 needed a third 'fast ship', as these supervessels were sometimes called. Of course, its greatest rival had plans of its own. The White Star Line was building the *Olympic*, then the *Titanic*, and had plans for the biggest of the trio, to be called *Gigantic*, but later renamed *Britannic*. But there were even greater worries, more serious threats, on the trans-Atlantic horizon. Germany's Hamburg America Line was planning the biggest liners of all, a trio of successively larger ships, the *Imperator*, then the *Vaterland* and finally the *Bismarck*. There was no question: Cunard had to keep pace and remain a very viable Atlantic liner company. Directors at Cunard's Liverpool headquarters opted for a ship some 15,000 tons larger than the *Lusitania* and *Mauretania*, one about 100 feet longer but with less powerful machinery. The trophy for trans-ocean speed would be left in the safe hands of the *Mauretania*. The new ship would copy the same four-funnel design (comparatively, the Germans would use three funnels) and, to many, to a better effect. Furthermore, Cunard opted to make her interiors more splendid.

John Brown & Company on the Clyde, which had built the *Lusitania*, got the job – they would build the new liner. Named *Aquitania* (for the Roman province in south-west France), it is one of the more beautiful names ever to put to sea. She was launched on 21 April 1913 and the company's three-liner express service would begin in the following May.

The *Aquitania* weighed in at 45,647 gross tons, measured 901 feet in length and was 97 feet wide. With her steam turbine machinery, she had four screws and could maintain a 23-knot service speed (using 680 tons of coal per day). Typically, she had three-class accommodations – 618 in First Class, 614 Second Class and, mostly for immigrants heading to America, 1,998 in Third Class.

Unfortunately, the *Aquitania* had barely entered Liverpool–New York service in May 1914 when the First World War dramatically erupted that summer. She was quickly called up for military service, first as an armed merchant cruiser, then a troopship and later as a hospital ship. While the likes of the *Lusitania, Mauretania* and *Aquitania* were intended from their earliest designs to be used as armed merchant cruisers in the event of war, it was quickly discovered that such big ships were actually very vulnerable to the sinister German U-boats. War Office ministers realised that they were better suited instead as high-capacity troopers.

The *Aquitania* also had an immediate cachet among Atlantic liners and was in the top tier of ocean-going royalty. Almost from the start, she was dubbed the 'Ship Beautiful'. This distinction lasted throughout her career, for thirty-five years, until 1949, and applied not only to her serene, almost perfectly balanced profile, but her splendid interiors as well. Surely, the columned Palladian lounge, which rose two decks in height, was one of the finest rooms ever to put to sea. Another was the Jacobean smoking room, which was copied from the Royal Naval College at Greenwich. In those high-spirited, pre-First World War days, it was quite common for designers and decorators to imitate shoreside structures – palaces, stately homes, even hunting lodges. Sometimes, there were even touches of the exotic – Arabian, Egyptian and Moorish themes.

After heroic war duties, the *Aquitania* was restored to her original luxurious self. The work was done at Newcastle, in 1919/20, and the opportunity taken to convert the liner from coal to oil fuel. The era of 200 or so stokers, the 'black gangs' as they were often called, was coming to a close – and aboard almost all other liners as well.

In the 1920s, the *Aquitania* settled down as an extremely popular and highly profitable liner. She was a proud member of Cunard's 'Big Three', sailing in tandem with the *Mauretania* and *Berengaria*. The *Aquitania* was noted among regular travellers for her gracious charm and for her reliability. Royalty and aristocracy, politicians and Hollywood stars were often photographed along her upper decks and in her lounges. In later years, she was not simply the 'Ship Beautiful' but also the 'Grand Old Lady'.

Serving on a ship such as the *Aquitania* as an officer or crewmember was, in ways, a great honour and a matter of pride. Cunard between the wars was one of the world's best known, most illustrious shipping companies on all the seas. Its superb reputation came not only from its big liners, but was based on its high shipboard standards, safety and punctuality. To be employed by Cunard was prestigious in itself. One officer later recalled, 'It was like working for the Bank of England.' Another officer from P&O added, 'When we saw a Cunard ship, say when entering a port or passing in the Channel, we sounded a salute on our whistle. It was a sort of curtsy to the greatness and high standard that Cunard represented.' A London-based ship designer once told me, 'Cunard taught us, more than any other company of its time, what great ships were supposed to be, what they should look like and how they should be run and maintained.' Crewmembers around the docks at London, Liverpool and Southampton often preferred working on Cunard liners.

All of these great ships had their share of mishaps, of course, and Cunarders were no exception. During the *Aquitania*'s post-war refit in 1919/20, there was an engine room explosion. One crewmember was killed. In the mid-1930s, she went aground twice – once at Calshot Spit for 2.5 hours and another time off Southampton for 26 hours. With 60 mph winds blowing and the removal of baggage and fuel oil, it took no less than eleven tugs to pull her free.

Changing times and economics affected the great Cunard passenger ships as well. Low-fare Third Class travel was often affected. In 1926, with US immigration quotas in place, Third Class quarters aboard the *Aquitania* were reduced from 1,998 to 640. In the early 1930s, with a new generation of art deco-styled liners arriving on the Atlantic run, the twenty-year-old *Aquitania* was taken in hand for some upgrading and modernisation. Among other touches, new suites were added to First Class. A Cunard press release noted:

You should see the new suites on the *Aquitania*. They're really quite extraordinary. They're really like charming guest rooms in delightful country homes. In fact, a few of these suites have private sun rooms in which the walls have been treated to resemble stone, carrying out the country house effect even further. Rooms have been larger, more beautiful and even some private baths and showers have been added.

In 1933, 1,000 shipyard workers toiled for three months to improve the aging liner. Afterward, she had an added amenity: a sound cinema. Hollywood films at sea!

Like almost all liners, the *Aquitania* struggled in the early 1930s of the Depression. Trans-Atlantic travel dropped by 50 per cent between 1930 and 1935. Now she sometimes crossed the Atlantic with just a few hundred passengers. Cunard opted to send her, similar to their other passenger ships, on cruises – some short, such as five and a half days to Bermuda or six days to Nassau from New York, six days from Southampton to Gibraltar, for as little as £5 (or $25) or, more luxuriously, two months to ports around the Mediterranean. She even had a month-long cruise to Rio de Janeiro for the Carnival celebrations.

By the mid-1930s, after the Cunard-White Star merger and when such liners as the *Mauretania*, *Olympic* and *Majestic* were being sold off, it was planned that the *Aquitania* would be withdrawn by 1940, just as the brand-new *Queen Elizabeth* was to enter commercial service between Southampton and New York. The *Aquitania* was paired for a time with the *Berengaria*, also aging, and the new *Queen Mary*. The late Everett Viez was employed as a travel agent in New York City at the time and remembered:

The *Queen Mary* was the big hit. Everyone wanted to sail in her, even in cheaper Third Class quarters. Ships like the *Aquitania* seemed very dated

by then, however. When visiting her on sailing days, I recall thinking that her interior decor, while interesting and well cared for, seemed as it came from another century. Art deco, the sleek modern on liners, was the big rage. Once I visited the *Queen Mary*, the fabulous *Normandie* and the *Aquitania* all in the same day. The *Aquitania*, always one of my favorite ships, seemed positively ancient in comparison.

The plan to retire the *Aquitania* in 1940, then the last four-stacker, never came about. When war between Britain and Nazi Germany broke out on 3 September 1939, thinking changed. The old *Aquitania* was needed for military duties. She was repainted in all grey to serve in her second conflict. Sometimes, in her voyages as far off as Sydney, she carried as many as 10,000 troops at a time. The late Charles Swanson was a soldier-passenger aboard the *Aquitania* in 1944. 'We crossed the Atlantic in very rough weather,' he told me.

Everyone was seasick. The ship rolled and shook and for seemed to be days. But I am not sure it was just the sea that made many of us ill. There was the awful smell, through the vents and ducts on deck, of foods – especially cabbage and boiled beef – prepared down in the ship's kitchens. It was the most wretched smell.

Even after the war ended in the summer of 1945, the *Aquitania* was still much needed. She was given a reprieve. She was pressed into Atlantic austerity service, sailing between Southampton and Halifax, with emigrants and returning troops and even the odd tourist. In the winter of 1950, she sailed to Faslane in Scotland to be broken up. After nearly thirty-six years, she was demolished not far from where she had been constructed.

Above: The splendid, 901-foot-long *Aquitania* departs from New York in this view dated 1922. (Richard K. Morse Collection)

Right: In dry dock, the four screws of the 45,647 grt *Aquitania* are clearly visible. (Norman Knebel Collection)

Above: Boom times: the busy Ocean Dock at Southampton – the *Homeric* and *Olympic* are on the left, the *Berengaria* and *Aquitania* to the right. (Cunard)

Right: Sail away! The splendid *Aquitania* sails off in this artist's rendition from the 1920s. (Norman Knebel Collection)

The Cunard company logo. (Norman Knebel Collection)

Above right: Comfort at sea: the drawing room and library aboard the 3,230-passenger *Aquitania*. (Norman Knebel Collection)

Right: Six courses for dinner – the First Class Louis XVI restaurant. The room was carpeted in a 'cool French blue' and the chairs upholstered in French tapestry. (Norman Knebel Collection)

Opposite: A listing of the Cunard fleet in 1925. (Norman Knebel Collection)

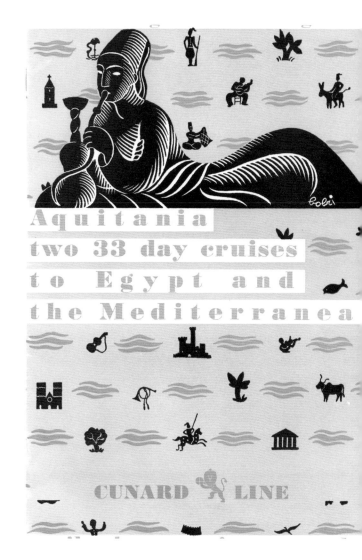

Left: An evocative depiction of the *Aquitania* used in a 1920s booklet on the ship's interiors. (Norman Knebel Collection)

Right: First Class only! Two thirty-three-day cruises to the Mediterranean in the 1930s. (Norman Knebel Collection)

AQUITANIA

CRUISE PLAN *and* RATE SCHEDULE

1937 CRUISE TO THE WEST INDIES AND

SOUTH AMERICA

VENEZUELA · BRAZIL · URUGUAY · ARGENTINA

from New York February 17, 1937

CUNARD WHITE STAR

Left: Exotic waters – a long, luxurious *Aquitania* cruise to South America in the winter of 1937. (Norman Knebel Collection)

Right: Superb artwork celebrating the *Aquitania*'s voyage to Latin American ports. (Norman Knebel Collection)

AQUITANIA
1937 WINTER CRUISE TO
SOUTH AMERICA

CUNARD WHITE STAR LINE

A Q U I T A N I A

In this long voyage you will be especially grateful for the great size of the Aquitania — her broad sports decks, and her indoor and outdoor swimming pools — her long promenades. Those who have rejoiced in her Atlantic crossings, will revel in an even wider range of pleasure beneath the tropic sun aboard the Aquitania.

Left: Cruising aboard the 'Ship Beautiful' – Cunard's long-lived *Aquitania*. (Norman Knebel Collection)

Right: Cruising elegance – high style and grand service aboard the all-one-class *Aquitania* during her winter cruises. (Norman Knebel Collection)

Left: Artist Donald Stoltenberg's evocative depiction of the much loved *Aquitania*. (Don Stoltenberg Collection)

Right: Advertising for a long, winter escape aboard the *Aquitania*. (National Geographic Society)

*Cruises
with the hallmark of*
CUNARD WHITE STAR

A FAMOUS STAR IN A DRAMATIC NEW ITINERARY!

The AQUITANIA
cruise de luxe to the West Indies and

SOUTH AMERICA
VENEZUELA · BRAZIL · URUGUAY · ARGENTINA
from New York Wednesday, February 17

Largest liner ever to sail below the Equator! Share the glory that will greet this famous star on her first appearance in glamorous Rio de Janeiro and Montevideo enjoy the fiestas of Buenos Aires at the peak of its summer season. Nine days in these three capitals a one river steamer to and from B. A. included in cruise rate. And you visit, too, Nassau and Panama, La Guaira, Barbados, Bahia, Trinidad. We suggest you make early reservations.

40 DAYS . . . $495 UP

SUNSHINE CRUISES
TO NASSAU AND THE CARIBBEAN

Britannic Christmas Cruise sails Dec. 18 to St. Thomas, La Guaira, Curaçao, Cartagena, Panama, Havana 15 days, $187.50 up.
Berengaria New Year's Cruise sails Dec. 29. New Year's Eve in Nassau! 5 days, $77.50 up.
Britannic to West Indies. 6-day cruise to Nassau Jan. 8, $75 up. 8 days to Nassau, Havana, sailing Jan. 16, $100 up.

Weekly Nassau Cruises Carinthia every Saturday Jan. 23 through Mar. 6-day round trip (day and evening in Nassau), $70 up. With stop-over privilege, $95 up. One way, $65 up.
Georgic to the Caribbean. Jan. 9 and 23 to Bermuda, Haiti, Havana, Nassau 11 days, $140 up. Feb. 6 and 27 to ten 'highspot' ports of the West Indies and South America. 18 days, $220 up.

Book through your local agent or Cunard White Star Line, 25 Broadway, and 638 Fifth Ave., N. Y.

THE BRITISH TRADITION DISTINGUISHES
CUNARD WHITE STAR

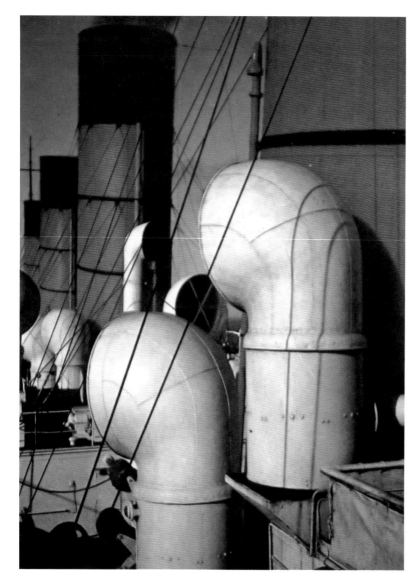

Above: Just after the end of the Second World War, in 1946, the troopship *Aquitania* visits Sydney, Australia. (Lindsay Johnstone Collection)

Left: Seen toward the end of her days, the *Aquitania* was the last of the four-stackers. (Richard Weiss Collection)

4. *SCYTHIA* (1920), *SAMARIA* (1921) AND *LACONIA* (1922)

A long-retired officer once told me that, as a young seaman with Cunard in the 1950s, he'd served on what were then the oldest passenger ships in the fleet: the *Scythia*, *Samaria*, *Franconia* and *Ascania*. They were thirty years old or more at the time and, as he described them, 'old and worn and quite tired'. They creaked, pipes burst and sometimes their old engines struggled to keep the posted schedules. As he told me, the captain of the *Franconia* dubbed the ship 'the Frankenstein'. She sometimes used to turn to port when the captain wanted to go to starboard and vice versa. Another captain dubbed the *Ascania* 'the Ashcan'. She too was old and tired and struggling.

The First World War had been cruel to Cunard. Eleven passenger ships – *Lusitania*, *Franconia*, *Alaunia*, *Ivernia*, *Laconia*, *Ultonia*, *Andania*, *Aurania*, *Ausonia*, *Ascania* and *Carpathia* – had been lost. Beginning soon after the Armistice in November 1918, restoration and especially replacement had been no easy task. Like a big Band-Aid, Cunard chartered relief passenger ships, some for as few as two or three voyages and others for a dozen or more. It was a diverse group from the likes of Union-Castle, Pacific Steam Navigation and Lamport & Holt. P&O's crack London–Bombay express ship, the *Kaisar-I-Hind* (advertised with the English translation of her name, *Emperor of India*), and Holland's *Prinses Juliana* were among those chartered for New York crossings.

After restoring its fast, luxury express service between Southampton, Cherbourg and New York, Cunard looked to reinforce its auxiliary services from Southampton as well as London and Liverpool to New York as well as Boston, Halifax and on the seasonal trade (April through December) to Quebec City and Montreal. Cunard's Liverpool-based directors also decided to build new passenger ships, but all of moderate size and modest speed. They were more practical, certainly very useful and sensibly economic. After all, the age of, say, mass emigration westbound to America was about to drop drastically (from 1 million migrants in 1914 to a scant 100,000 by 1924) because of new quotas begun in 1922. Therefore, it was projected that these new ships would rely more on general tourist traffic, passengers who wanted less luxury and high speed, but comfort and reliability and all at reasonable fares. And so, Cunard embarked on a very ambitious rebuilding program – fourteen new passenger liners in all. (There was one misfit, however, the 12,700 grt *Albania*, a passenger-cargo liner that carried only eighty passengers and which was retired after only five years of Cunard service and later sold off.)

The first five passenger ships began with the 1920-built *Samaria* and two identical sisters, the *Scythia* (1921) and *Laconia* (1922). Two modified near-sisters followed: the *Franconia* of 1923 and the *Carinthia* of 1925. Built by Cammell, Laird & Company at Birkenhead, along the Mersey and near Liverpool, the *Samaria* weighed in at 19,602 gross tons, was 624 feet in length and 73 feet wide. She was propelled by steam turbines and was twin-screw, making a 16-knot service speed. As built, her quarters were arranged for 2,190 passengers – 350 First Class, 340 Second and 1,500 Third.

Cruising, seeing places by ship but for leisure rather than a purpose, began only slowly in the nineteenth century. It would grow steadily by the 1920s and more so in the otherwise troubled 1930s. The New York-based American Express was among those that saw potential in leisure cruising, especially in the winter off-season when Atlantic passengers dropped, and so planned the first continuous around-the-world cruise. They chartered the *Laconia* from Cunard for a 130-day voyage, departing on 21 November and returning on 30 March. There would be twenty-two ports in the circumnavigation. It was beginning of full world cruises. Millionaires, especially in America, loved these voyages. The *Laconia*, with her capacity reduced to a club-like 450 passengers only, preceded the next three world cruise departures, heading off in January 1923, aboard the *Samaria*, *Resolute* and *Empress of France*. The *Laconia* and *Samaria* would actually meet in the Indian Ocean.

The *Laconia*'s itinerary went in a westward direction. The ports of call included Havana, Colón and the Panama Canal, Cape St Louis (Mexico), Catalina Island, San Francisco, Hilo (Hawaii), Honolulu, Yokohama, Kobe, Damien, Tsingtao, Shanghai, Cheking, Hong Kong, Manila, Java, Singapore, Rangoon, Calcutta, Colombo, Bombay, Port Sudan, Port Tewfik, Alexandria, Naples, Monte Carlo, Gibraltar and then a return to New York. American Express presented the master of the *Laconia* with the so-called Laconia Cup, which today is aboard the *Queen Victoria*. After the *Laconia*'s inaugural world cruise, the world voyage was assigned to the *Franconia*.

The *Samaria* and *Scythia* were often used for Cunard cruises from New York in the Depression-era early 1930s. One newspaper advertisement read:

> Cap Haitien, Cartagena, Curaçao, San Juan, St Pierre, Barbados, Port of Spain, La Guaira, Nassau, St Thomas, Santo Domingo, Port au Prince, Fort de France, Havana. Magic, romantic, exciting names ... on Cunard's unusual West Indies itineraries this season ... lavish entertainments ... deck sports ... dances ... and don't forget to come prepared for the costume party. The *Scythia* departing on February 27th [1932] for 23 days with fares from $225 and up; or the same ship on April 16th for 12 days from $120 and up.

The *Laconia* was a casualty of the Second World War, being torpedoed and sunk in the South Atlantic in September 1942. It was in fact a horrific loss – over 2,500 perished, including 1,800 Italian prisoners-of-war. The *Scythia* and *Samaria* survived the war and were restored (with much reduced capacities) but primarily for Cunard's service to eastern Canada and were finally broken up in Scotland in 1956 and 1958 respectively.

Above: Preparing to sail – the 19,860 grt *Laconia* seen at Liverpool. (Cunard)

Right: Cunard's more modest class of single-stack, 20,000-tonners were added in the early 1920s. (Norman Knebel Collection)

Great modern luxury ships

Carinthia
Franconia
Laconia
Scythia
Samaria
Lancastria

Cunard

Left: The palm
court for the
337 First Class
passengers aboard
the 1921-built
Scythia. (Norman
Knebel Collection)

Right: Cruising
with Cunard in
1927/28. (National
Geographic
Society)

THE RAYMOND-WHITCOMB ROUND SOUTH AMERICA CRU

See ALL South America—

INCA towns of unknown antiquity and brilliant twentieth-century capitals—Indians in gaudy ponchos and black-eyed Spanish-Americans in Paris gowns—snowy Andes and green jungles—vast pampas and narrow fjords—*Arequipa, Lima, Santiago, Valparaiso,* and *Valdivia;* the coveted *Nitrate Country* and the *Straits of Magellan; Buenos Aires, Montevideo, Rio de Janeiro, Santos, Sao Paulo* and *Bahia.*

Two Months of Luxurious Tra

THE Cunard liner *"Laconia"*—large and luxurious—special chartered by RAYMOND-WHITCOMB—will make the enti cruise, from New York back to New York, in two months. There wi be no changing of ships—no delays or wasted time—no continu packing and unpacking; but instead a carefully planned voyage on single splendid steamship, with visits to the famous historic places an great cities of South America & a rich program of sight-seeing ashor

The Only Real South America Cruise

THIS is the only Cruise to see more of South America than three or four East Coast cities—or to see any of the West Coast. (And to omit the West Coast is to miss one of the most characteristic parts of the continent.) To know South America you must see it all—North and South, East and West—for it is a land of strong contrasts and marked extremes and no single section of it is typical of the whole.

Sailing January 29, 1927   Rates, $975 and upward   Send for the booklet, "Round South America" & Ship Pla

Other Raymond-Whitcomb Cruises

The West Indies, January 27 & February 22 ∾ The Mediterranean, February 9 & March 29
The North Cape, June 28 ∾ Round the World, January 18, 1928 ∾ Round Africa, January 14, 1
Land Cruises to California—December to April

RAYMOND & WHITCOMB COMPAI

Executive Offices: 26 Beacon Street, Boston, Massachusetts

NEW YORK   PHILADELPHIA   CHICAGO   LOS ANGELES   SAN FRAN

LACONIA

LIVERPOOL OVERHEAD RAILWAY

A ROUND TRIP 13 MILES GIVES UNRIVALLED VIEWS of DOCKLAND & SHIPPING

FIRST CLASS 1/. THIRD CLASS 9D

PERMITS TO INSPECT LINERS SOLD AT PIERHEAD & JAMES ST. STATIONS

FOR ALL PARTICULARS APPLY W.I. BOX, GENERAL MANAGER. 11 JAMES ST. LIVERPOOL.

Above: The funnel aboard the 624-foot-long *Laconia* is made larger by the artist to give the ship added might and security. (Author's Collection)

Right: The famed Liverpool Overhead Railway was popular for seeing passenger ships, including Cunarders. (Author's Collection)

FORM B 89.

TOURIST THIRD CABIN

CUNARD LINE
NEW YORK - HAVRE SERVICE

DISEMBARKATION CARD

No. on List _208_.

S.S. _SCYTHIA_ sailing _18:5:1927_

Mr. _Percy H. Davies_

Ticket No. _777423_

TO BE PRESENTED TO THE IMMIGRATION OFFICER IN EXCHANGE FOR A LANDING CARD

19/9317

Above: Disembarkation card from the *Scythia*, dated 8 September 1927. (Author's Collection)

Right: Daily programme aboard the *Scythia* in her later years, dated 21 June 1950. (Author's Collection)

ORCHESTRAL SELECTIONS
DIRECTED BY JACK GELLER.
Violin Lead   -   -   Jack Davis.

At 11-00 a.m.

Paso Doble	" ESPANOLA "	Winkler
Selection	" GLAMOROUS NIGHTS "	Novello
Waltz	" LOVE'S LAST WORD IS SPOKEN "	Bixio
Entr'acte	" COMEDIAN'S GALOP "	Kabalevsky
Serenade	" NEAPOLITAN "	Winkler
Signature	" CAREFREE "	Geller

At 4-45 p.m.

Paso Doble	" LADY OF MADRID "	Evans
Waltz	" IM CHAMBRE SEPAREE "	Henberger
Selection	" MAID OF THE MOUNTAINS "	Simpson
'Cello Solo (by Fred Baines)	" PHANTOM MELODY "	Ketelby
Descriptive	" BLACK EYES "	Traditional
Signature	" CAREFREE "	Geller

MEAL HOURS

BREAKFAST	- 1st Sitting	8-00 a.m.	2nd Sitting	9-00 a.m.
LUNCHEON	- ,,	12-15 p.m.	,,	1-30 p.m.
DINNER	- ,,	6-30 p.m.	,,	7-45 p.m.

BAGGAGE

Several Passengers are being inconvenienced by Missing Baggage. Will Passengers please check their baggage and inform the Bedroom Steward or Stewardess of any piece which does not belong in their Cabin.

R.M.S. "SAMARIA"

PROGRAMME OF EVENT
(Subject to Alteration)

WEDNESDAY, 21st JUNE, 195(

8-00 a.m	Deck Games available	Spo
10-00 a.m.	Passenger Boat Drill (Life Jackets to Passengers are earnestly requested to attend this	
11-00 a.m.	Orchestral Selections	Main
4-00 p.m.	Afternoon Tea Served on Deck, in Public Rooms and " D " Deck Dining Rooms (Forwa	
4-30 p.m.	Cinema Cinema Hall, " D " De " JOHNNY BELINDA " Featuring :—Jane Wyman, Lew Ayres and Charle Repeat Performances at 8-30 to-night an to-morrow at 9-45 a,m., 1-30 &	
4-45 p.m.	Tea Time Music	Main
6-00 p.m.	Cocktail Hour	Star'd Garden
8-30 p.m.	Cinema Cinema Hall, " D " De REPEAT PERFORMANCE	
9-00 p.m.	Horse Racing	Main
10-00 p.m.	Dancing Port Garden Lounge, Pr (Weather Permitting)	

5. LANCASTRIA (1922)

Television documentaries about the Second World War were in abundance by the 1990s. Often very rare film footage was used and was usually accompanied by on-camera recollections from soldiers, ex-prisoners and survivors of disasters. One of these involved one of the worst maritime tragedies, not only of that war but of all time. It involved the sinking of Cunard's *Lancastria*, which – while being used as a troopship for the hurried evacuation of western France in June 1940 – was attacked by Nazi bombers. She sank within 20 minutes. There were, it was estimated, as many as 5,000 casualties.

Completed as the *Tyrrhenia* in the summer of 1922, this 578-foot-long liner differed in design from the other Cunard intermediate ships of the time. She was in fact a half-sister to Anchor Line's *Cameronia*, having been designed for that Glasgow-based firm just before the First World War. She was transferred to Cunard just after the Armistice, in late 1918. Her Anchor name was not popular, however, and often mispronounced and even hard to spell. Some dubbed the *Tyrrhenia* as 'the soup tureen'. The name was even disliked by the rather notorious Liverpool dockers. By 1924, the 16,243 grt ship had been renamed *Lancastria*. Built by

William Beardmore & Company at Glasgow, she was fitted out to carry up to 1,846 passengers – 235 in First Class, 355 Second and 1,256 Third.

Hard hit by the passenger-declining 1930s, she avoided being laid up by offering bargain cruises to the likes of Bermuda, Nassau and the Caribbean, as well as from British ports. Her hull was repainted in heat-resistant all-white. A particular six-day voyage in May 1935 must have been a very special occasion, when she ran a cruise that included 'spectator' participation in the King George V's Silver Jubilee Fleet Review off Spithead.

Called to duty as a troopship in the autumn of 1939, the *Lancastria's* end was one of the most tragic in maritime history. She was selected to participate in the evacuation of refugees from western France. As the French forces surrendered to the advancing Nazis, the *Lancastria* arrived at St Nazaire on 17 June 1940 and took aboard over 5,000 evacuees including large numbers of women and children. Shortly afterward, she was attacked by enemy bombers. The first bomb went through her funnel and then exploded in the engine room; the two others fell into the cargo holds and blew out the sides of the ship. Survivors reported

Cunard

"Lancastria" Holiday Cruises
from 9 guineas — 1933 — One Class Only

that the *Lancastria* seemed to jump out of the water. She sank within 20 minutes with the loss of over 3,000 lives. The tragedy was considered by many, including Winston Churchill himself, to be so demoralising that its full details were withheld for five years, until the first summer of peace, in 1945.

LANCASTRIA

Above: The 16,243 grt *Lancastria*, completed in 1922, had been built initially as Anchor Line's *Tyrrhernia*. (Author's Collection)

Left: Cruising from 9 guineas in 1933 aboard the *Lancastria*. (Cunard)

6. ANTONIA (1921), AUSONIA (1921), ANDANIA (1922), AURANIA (1924), ALAUNIA (1925) AND ASCANIA (1925)

'It was the voyage of my lifetime. I had never even seen the sea, but my family and I headed [by train] to Liverpool, where we caught the *Ascania*,' recalled Gregory Chisholm.

We were leaving Lancashire, heading for a new life in Canada. It was the 1950s and life in Britain was still very gray. There was still the lingering cloud, economically and socially, of the Second World War. I had read about giant liners such as the *Queen Mary*, but to me, the *Ascania* was a giant liner as well. We climbed aboard at the Landing Stage in Liverpool and, although we were down in lower-deck tourist class, that old ship seemed like a fancy hotel: lounges, a library and folded white linen napkins in the dining room. I watched from the deck as we sailed off – and then watched as England itself disappeared in the gray clouded murkiness of an autumn day. It took over a week to cross before we entered the wide mouth of the St Lawrence River and I had my first glimpse of Canada, our new home. Even though I later discovered it was quite a small liner, the *Ascania* was the 'bridge'. I shall never ever forget that voyage aboard that Cunard ship.

The design of the 20,000-ton *Scythia* and her two sisters was reworked at the time of their construction, changed, modified and then reduced as the six sisters of the 14,000-ton 'A Class' – ships that would be named *Antonia*, *Ausonia* and *Andania* (all 1922) and then the *Aurania*, *Ascania* and *Alaunia* (1924/25).

Smaller and less impressive than, say, the *Scythia* class, these ships were even more functional: a clear division between upper-deck Cabin Class (beds for 484 on the *Antonia*) and a far more austere Third Class (1,222 berths, also on the *Antonia*) plus a large cargo capacity. They were, in ways, the ideal little Atlantic liners that could be assigned easily amid Cunard's Atlantic services – summer seasons to Quebec City and Montreal, winters to Halifax or to New York. They could also be used for cruising. They established enviable reputations for fine Cunard service and comfortable quarters. On board the 540-foot-long *Antonia*, for example, the Cabin Class smoking room was done in Adam style, the lounge in Louis XIV style. The restaurant ran the full width of the ship. Overall, these 15-knot, steam turbine-driven ships had an unpretentious appearance with a single funnel, twin masts, counter stern and seven sets of lifeboats.

The eventual fates of these six A Class liners were varied. The *Andania* was sunk by a German U-boat off Reykjavik, Iceland, in June 1940. The *Ascania* survived the war, which included her participation in the invasion of Sicily in July 1943, was restored (in 1949/50) for mostly Canadian passenger service (and far fewer passengers) and then was retired and scrapped in 1957. Four of the others were subsequently sold to the British Admiralty. Because of the great shortage of specialty tonnage, they were rebuilt as Royal Navy fleet-repair ships and floating workshops. The *Antonia*, which had carried 2,000 British soldiers to Iceland, which, it was thought, would be invaded by the Nazis, in October 1940, became HMS *Wayland* in 1944 and was scrapped four years later in Scotland. The *Aurania* – which collided with an iceberg in the North Atlantic in July 1941 and then was torpedoed three months later – became HMS *Artifax*, also in 1944, and endured until Italian scrappers bought her in 1961. The *Alaunia* as HMS *Alaunia* was broken up at Blyth in Scotland in 1957. Finally, the *Ausonia* was restyled as the HMS *Ausonia* and served at Malta for many years. She was decommissioned in 1964 and scrapped a year later in Spain. By then, she was the last survivor of this class of Cunarders.

Above: Painted all white: the *Lancastria* was a very popular cruise ship. The 578-foot-long ship is seen here berthed on the north side of Pier 90, New York, and with three of the *Aquitania*'s four funnels just behind. This photo dates from June 1939. (Author's Collection)

Right: The *Antonia* was one of Cunard's smaller 'A Class' of little liners created in the early twenties. (Alex Duncan)

Above: The *Andania* sailing from New York's Pier 54, at the foot of West 13th Street. (Cunard)

Right: The late Keith Byass's painting of the *Andania* being docked at Southampton. (Author's Collection)

Above: Deck games aboard the *Ascania* in the 1930s. (Author's Collection)

Right: The upper deck aboard the *Ascania* in a view dated 1955. (Steffen Weirauch Collection)

7. FRANCONIA (1923) AND CARINTHIA (1925)

The Museum of the North Atlantic, the maritime museum at Halifax, Nova Scotia, has a wonderful collection. Among the items are several of those great, oversized models. In September 2004, during the maiden calls there of the *Queen Mary 2*, there was a new addition. It was Cunard's white-hulled *Franconia* of 1923. The model had long been lost, but then was uncovered in a Toronto basement. Cunard itself had long ago given away the model but, quite happily, it was again to see the light of day. Donated to the museum in Halifax and then transported there by truck, the 12-foot-long recreation first needed extensive surgery and renewal. It needed a thorough cleaning and many of the details – from small anchor chains to wind scoops on deck to the tiniest of lifeboat pulleys – needed to be refitted and sometimes replaced. A team of very competent volunteer model-makers spent hundreds of hours on that Cunard model. It was about to formally appear in the museum's gallery when we visited from the *Queen Mary 2*. Commodore Ron Warwick, master of the then-new Cunard flagship, was invited to visit the museum and, rather informally, unveil the restored *Franconia* model. As we arrived, work was almost complete.

The repainted, restored single stack had not yet been secured, however. This created a great photo opportunity: Commodore Warwick holding the funnel above the model itself.

The 20,158 grt *Franconia*, completed in June 1923, and her twin sister, the 623-foot-long *Carinthia* (actually intended to be the *Servia*), delivered two summers later, were improved versions of the *Scythia* and her two sisters. There were exterior as well as structural differences and both were better decorated, more luxurious. While they were intended for class-divided but seasonal service between Liverpool, Cobh and New York, it was intended from the start that they would also cruise for as much as half the year. Early on, Cunard was insightful: the company saw tremendous potential in cruising. Not only was there potential in one- to three-week-long voyages to Bermuda, Nassau and the Caribbean islands from New York or for two to three weeks to the Canaries and Madeira or within the Mediterranean from Southampton, London and Liverpool, but on long luxurious itineraries: eight weeks around South America, six weeks to Scandinavia, two months around Africa and, most luxurious of all, four- and five-month-long circumnavigations of the globe. World cruises on both the *Franconia* and *Carinthia* became legendary in 1930s travel circles, in fact.

An advertisement for the *Carinthia*'s autumn 1925 world cruise read:

Sails from New York 10th October, Los Angeles 25th October and San Francisco 27th October. Visits Cuba, Panama, Hawaii, Japan, China, the Philippines, New Guinea, New Zealand, Australia, Java, Singapore, India, Egypt, Italy, France and England. Ending at Southampton 10th March. 38,000 miles ... 149 days (and nights) of cruising ... visiting 51 ports in 21 countries and colonies. The brand new *Carinthia*, the finest of Cunarders, has unique equipment: Instantaneous running hot water in every cabin, beds six inches wider than on other ships, exceptional deck space, squash court and pool. All for $2,000 upward.

Built to carry up to 1,843 passengers on her Atlantic crossings (221 First Class, 336 Second Class and 1,266 Third Class), the *Franconia* and *Carinthia*'s cruising capacity was kept to a club-like 400. She had splendid quarters: a two-deck-high smoking room that was styled after the fifteenth-century residence of El Greco; another lounge done in Early English style; twin garden lounges; and such special amenities as a chocolate shop, health centre and even a racquetball court.

The *Carinthia* also did extra service in 1930. She was chartered to the Furness-Bermuda Line for six-day New York–Bermuda voyages. Furness had just lost their liner *Bermuda* to fire and were in urgent need of a replacement. The *Franconia* was similarly chartered, but for the 1931 Bermuda season.

Both the *Franconia* and *Carinthia* were re-painted in heat-resistant white in 1933 and 1935 respectively. They now not only resembled large luxury yachts but appeared more tropical. By then, the two ships were running cruises almost fulltime and these included shorter voyages as well. In the

winter of 1937/38, for example, the *Carinthia* ran weekly seven-day cruises between New York and Nassau, departing on Saturday afternoons.

The glamour of midnight suppers on trans-Atlantic crossings and cruise calls at such exotic places as Acapulco, Bali and Bombay were pushed aside by September 1939. Britain was at war and the 16½-knot *Franconia* hurriedly repainted in all gray and outfitted to carry as many as 3,000 troops. Promptly dispatched to the Mediterranean, she collided on 5 October with another large trooper, Royal Mail's *Alcantara*. Soon repaired, the *Franconia* had a further incident: in June 1940, she was hit in an air attack during the evacuation of western France. The *Carinthia* was far less fortunate, however. She was torpedoed by a Nazi submarine and sunk off the Irish coast in June 1940.

The *Franconia* was called to special duty in the winter of 1945. Some of her luxury fittings were pulled out of storage, fitted aboard in a special section and the ship ordered to the Mediterranean for 'top secret duty'. She was sent to Yalta, to serve as the floating headquarters for Prime Minister Winston Churchill and his staff during the historic Yalta Conference. A series of suites were arranged for the official party as well as dining and meeting facilities. A staff of over 100 accompanied Mr Churchill and this included secretaries, typists, telegraphers and, of course, security staff.

After the war, following a full refit in 1948/49, the *Franconia*'s accommodation was greatly reduced – to 853 passengers in total (253 First Class, 600 Tourist Class). She was used as part of the revival of Cunard's seasonal Canadian service – between Liverpool, Greenock and Quebec City. In winter, when the St Lawrence was ice-clogged, she was detoured from Liverpool and Cobh to Halifax and New York. Her schedules even included a Caribbean cruise from New York in 1956. Her later days were not without incident, however. On 14 July 1950, just a mile downriver from Quebec City, she went aground. In deepening old age, her steering gear had grown faulty. All the passengers were sent ashore and then, unable to lighten the ship and free it, crew members were sent aboard to pack and then offload passengers' baggage. In the end, it took four weeks and a half dozen tugs to free her. She had temporary repairs at nearby Sorel, re-crossed the Atlantic and then had full repairs in a UK shipyard.

With the arrival of new liners for the Canadian run – a 22,000-ton quartet named *Saxonia*, *Ivernia*, *Carinthia* and *Sylvania* (1954–57) – the thirty-three-year-old *Franconia* was finally sold for breaking-up in 1956.

Awaiting her passengers: the *Franconia* anchored in the Mersey. (J. K. Byass)

Looking like a white yacht, the 624-foot-long *Carinthia* in the Mersey. (Cronican-Arroyo Collection)

CARINTHIA

Above: Tropical morning: the *Carinthia* anchored in a Mediterranean port. (Author's Collection)

Right: Cruising including Cunard in 1928. (National Geographic Society)

Come where the summer
days are three months long—
ON THE RAYMOND WHITCOMB

North Cape Cruise

Sail with the luxuries of a great liner
to the interesting countries of northern
Europe that few travelers know:

Norway with its wonderful Fjords
Stockholm and ruined Visby in Sweden
Copenhagen and Danzig
Iceland island of geysers and glaciers

*The Cruise will visit Russia also — for
two days in Moscow the capital, and two
more in Leningrad, at no additional cost*

It will be very easy to follow the Cruise with travel
in England, France, or Germany. It calls at Havre
and Southampton and the rates include return passage to America at any time. $800 and upward.

To sail June 30 on the S. S. "Carinthia"

For ten years the favorite summer Cruise

Send for the booklet — "The North Cape and Russia"

Tours to Europe $950 to $2860
Summer Tours to the National Parks
California, Alaska and Mexico
Independent Trips in Europe or America
For Next Winter
South America — West Indies Cruise
Mediterranean Cruise

Raymond & Whitcomb Co.

126 Newbury Street, Boston, Massachusetts

New York, 670 Fifth Avenue; New York, 225 Fifth Avenue.
Boston, 165 Tremont Street ; Philadelphia, 1601 Walnut St.
Chicago, 176 N. Michigan Ave.; Detroit, 421 Book Bldg.
Los Angeles, 423 West Fifth St.; San Francisco, 230 Post St.

Agents in the principal cities

phic—It identifies you."

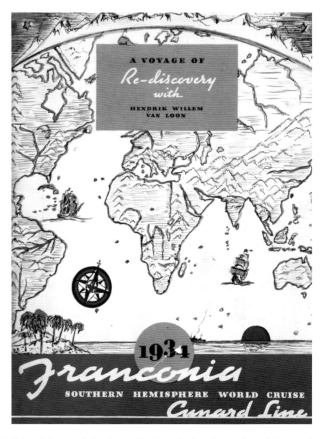

Left: Off to the North Cape, the Norwegian fjords, the Baltic cities and Leningrad aboard the *Carinthia*. (National Geographic Society)

Middle: Another wonderful cover for a Cunard long-cruise booklet. (Norman Knebel Collection)

Right: The long, luxurious Southern Hemisphere World Cruise for the *Franconia* in 1934. (Norman Knebel Collection)

CARINTHIA

PLAN of

TOURIST CLASS

DATE OF ISSUE
APRIL 1938
REVISION OF
JULY 1936 ISSUE

FORM C 270
T. T. C. 95037

BOOK THRU YOUR LOCAL AGENT
NO ONE CAN SERVE YOU BETTER

CUNARD WHITE STAR LINE

25 BROADWAY
638 FIFTH AVENUE
NEW YORK CITY
OFFICES AND AGENCIES EVERYWHERE

PRINTED IN U.S.A.

Right: A Tourist Class
deck plan for the 20,227
grt *Carinthia*. (Norman
Knebel Collection)

Far right: Summer to
the North Cape aboard
the *Franconia*. (Norman
Knebel Collection)

NORTH CAPE-RUSSIA CRUISE

To the Land of the

Midnight

Sun

In the
CUNARD
WHITE STAR
LINER
"Franconia"
1937

RAYMOND • WHITCOMB

Left: Another long cruise with Cunard. (Norman Knebel Collection)

Far left: Seventy-five days and nights to South America, Africa and the Mediterranean aboard the *Carinthia*. (Norman Knebel Collection)

Above: The sailings of Anchor Line passenger ships were coordinated and marketed by Cunard. Here we see the 17,046 grt, 1,408-passenger *Caledonia* berthed at Glasgow. (Michael Cassar)

Right: Six-day cruises from New York to Nassau and with fares from $55 aboard the *Lancastria*. (Norman Knebel Collection)

Above: The sailings of Glasgow-headquartered Donaldson Line were also marketed by Cunard. Here we see Donaldson's *Letitia*, but shown in her later years, in the 1950s, as the migrant ship *Captain Cook*. (Author's Collection)

Left: Cruising aboard the likes of the *Tuscania, Aurania* and *Caledonia*. (National Geographic Society)

8. ADRIATIC (1906)

They were known as the 'Big Four' – two sets of sisters, the *Celtic* (1901) and *Cedric* (1903), and then the *Baltic* (1904) and *Adriatic* (1907). All but the 24,541 grt *Adriatic* were, for short periods, the world's largest liner. In their day, they were the 'crack ships' in the White Star fleet. They were rather conservative ships, however, and best exemplified by each having four tall masts, which were intended to remind the public of the glorious sailing ships of the previous century. Overall, the Big Four had a strong, sound image – they were comfortable, reliable and never intended to break any Atlantic speed record. They worked the Liverpool–New York trade with a weekly departure in each direction.

Each of these ships survived the ordeals and even dangers of the First World War and resumed White Star sailings in the 1920s. The *Celtic* was stranded and lost in December 1928, however. After all salvage attempts failed, she was declared a constructive loss. She was sold to Danish salvagers and the final wreckage was not cleared until 1933. Over sixty-five years later, during a positioning cruise from Southampton to Montreal in September 2014, we called in at the great Irish port of Cobh. Our visit included a meeting with Oliver Hawes, the local World Ship Society chairman. In his good care, we were off to Cork, to the Long Valley pub, to see the furniture and wood panelling taken from the *Celtic*. 'After running aground, it took five years to demolish the wreckage,' said Hawes. 'Afterward, there was a huge auction. Every house in Cork had something from the *Celtic*. But the best of it all went to the Long Valley pub.' There were doors, stained glass, tables, chairs and benches. Later, we drove out to seaside Bunnyconnellan, overlooking the site where another White Star liner, the *Titanic*, was anchored and afterward set off on her ill-fated maiden voyage.

The three survivors – *Cedric*, *Baltic* and *Adriatic* – soon faced hard times and, within the struggling White Star fleet, were among the first victims of the Depression. The *Cedric* went to Scottish ship breakers in January 1932, her sale price being just over £22,000 ($107,000) and was much needed to help restore the falling White Star coffers. A year later, with the Japanese offering better prices, the *Baltic* left Liverpool under her own power and later was delivered to demolition crews at Osaka. The *Adriatic* lingered on. By then in her twilight, the 24,541 grt, 726-foot-long ship was listed as having a capacity of 1,470 passengers – 506 Cabin Class, 560 Tourist Class and 404 Third Class.

Soon after the Cunard-White Star merger in April 1934, the twenty-seven-year-old, Belfast-built ship was placed on the disposal list. Between short periods of lay-up, she spent her final season on inexpensive, pound-a-day cruises and also under charter to the British Boy Scouts Association, ferrying youngsters on short exploration cruises. But by that November, she was laid up for good. With the Japanese still offering attractive scrap metal prices, she too sailed east. In the end, the *Adriatic* fetched £62,000 ($177,000). She was handed over at Osaka in March 1935, by then the oldest liner in the former White Star fleet and the last of the famous Big Four. At the time, White Star Line seemed to be losing all of its ships and very rapidly.

The last of White Star's 'Big Four', the *Adriatic*, at the Princes Landing Stage, Liverpool. (Cunard)

9. OLYMPIC (1911)

In October 2008, a cruise aboard the *Queen Elizabeth 2*, itself then nearing her retirement with Cunard, included a call at Newcastle. It was the iconic, thirty-nine-year-old ship's 'Farewell to the British Isles' cruise. Newcastle, a well rejuvenated and revived city by then, had much changed. The famed 'coals from Newcastle', for example, were by then imported, in fact as much as 90 per cent from Poland. And the last of the famous shipyards, Swan Hunter (builders of such liners as the legendary *Mauretania* of 1907), had closed down the year before and, symptomatic of many British shipyards, was reduced to memory. Most of the towering cranes and other equipment were later sold and carted off to India.

On a ship's afternoon excursion, I travelled to Alnwick, about 30 miles away, to see the local castle, owned and still occupied by the Duke and Duchess of Northumberland. But it was actually a spin-off visit: I was really off on my own for a bit, into the village to see the White Swan Hotel. The smallish hotel has an ocean liner connection: the dining room and lounge include fine wood panelling taken from the liner *Olympic*, sister ship to the immortal *Titanic*. The *Olympic* had been scrapped locally, over seventy years before, at nearby Jarrow in 1936. Along with the scrap metal,

the wood was sold off to raise money in those hard-pressed Depression-era times. Pristine and polished and balanced by fine stained glass windows, the spaces were flooded by great autumn afternoon sunlight. The hotel space is splendid and indeed well worth the visit.

In the 1920s, White Star publicists went to considerable lengths to avoid any and all reminders that the *Olympic* was actually an earlier sister of the ill-fated *Titanic*. For the most part, the 46,439 grt *Olympic* – built by Harland & Wolff at Belfast – had a charmed life and was certainly one of the most popular liners of her time. She was dubbed 'Old Reliable' by the troops that sailed in her during the First World War. Her wartime record included a heroic attempt to tow a stricken British battleship to safety and the sinking of a German U-boat. Even in peacetime, there were auspicious events: in September 1912, she collided with a British cruiser and, in May 1934, sank the Nantucket Lightship off New York harbour.

The four-funnel, 882-foot-long *Olympic* carried up to 1,447 passengers in 1932, two years before the Cunard-White Star merger. This was divided between 618 First Class, 447 Tourist Class and 382 Third

Class. She was hard-hit, however, by the Depression and slump in trans-Atlantic travel. She often arrived in New York with as few as 500 passengers. In the end, she was demoted, being sent off on pound-a-day Bank Holiday cruises from Southampton and three-night trips up to Halifax from New York. Deficit-ridden, she was laid up in the spring of 1935. While Mussolini's government eyed her for possible troopship service with their East African campaign, she was sold to Sir John Jarvis for £100,000 ($147,000), but he resold her and for the same amount to British shipbreakers Thomas Ward & Company Limited. Under the provisions of the sales contract, she had to be broken up at Jarrow to alleviate chronic unemployment in the north-east of England. Cut down to the double bottom, her final remains were towed to Scotland and scrapped a year later.

Above: Departing from New York's Chelsea Piers, crowds see off the 882-foot-long *Olympic*. (Cronican-Arroyo Collection)

Right: Royal travellers: Lord and Lady Mountbatten finishing a North American tour with a sailing from New York aboard the *Olympic*. The view is dated 22 December 1922. (Author's Collection)

Opposite: A busy day at Southampton in 1934: the *Aquitania, Berengaria, Olympic* and Orient Line's *Orontes* are in the Ocean Dock (centre); the *Alcantara* and *Strathaird* are in the lower right; the *Lancastria* and *Arandora Star* are in the lower left; and in the upper left are the *Mauretania* and *Empress of Britain*. (Author's Collection)

Above: Clarence H. Mackay, president of the Postal Telegraph, and his wife return from Europe aboard the *Olympic* in a scene dated 15 September 1923. (Author's Collection)

Left: Another of artist Donald Stoltenberg's fine views of great liners. The *Olympic* is shown at Southampton. (Donald Stoltenberg Collection)

Off and away on a cruise in the early 1930s, the flag-bedecked *Olympic* sails from Southampton. (F. W. Hawks)

10. HOMERIC (1914–22)

Like Cunard, White Star Line produced some very lavish brochures and booklets for its ships and also for their long, luxurious cruises. Among the finest were those for the *Homeric*, which by the early 1930s was making some of White Star's finest cruises. Topped by very attractive, often very colourful, covers, the inner pages contained oversized photos of the ship's accommodations, life aboard and the often exotic ports of call. The *Homeric* was indeed one of the great luxury cruise ships of the early 1930s.

The 774-foot-long *Homeric* had been ordered in 1913 as the *Columbus* for the North German Lloyd. To avoid subsequent confusion, a sister ship, the intended *Hindenburg*, was in fact retained by the Germans after the First World War and was completed, in 1924, as the 'second' *Columbus*.

In 1919, after Allied reparation settlements were made, the original yet still incomplete *Columbus* was given to White Star. As the new owners, White Star promptly sent a team of engineers and designers to Schichau shipyard at Danzig to supervise the ship's completion. In service by the winter of 1922, the 34,352-ton ship joined White Star's 'Big Three' in service between Southampton, Cherbourg and New York. She was partnered with the larger *Majestic* and *Olympic*, and in direct competition in express

service with Cunard's *Mauretania*, *Aquitania* and *Berengaria*. White Star publicists wanted a separate identity for the 19-knot, twin-screw *Homeric* and, because of her strong, solid construction, she gained a reputation as one of the 'steadiest' liners on the Atlantic.

Carrying 2,766 passengers (529 First, 487 Second and 1,750 Third), the otherwise smartly appointed *Homeric* had a comparatively short trans-Atlantic life. In just ten years, by June 1932, she became one of the first White Star liners to be used solely for cruising. Business on the Atlantic had fallen considerably and cruising was the ship's economic alternative. Mostly, she went off on two-week cruises, usually from Liverpool or Southampton to the Canaries, West Africa, Spain and Portugal, and sometimes, on three-week voyages, into the Mediterranean. Previously, in the late 1920s, she had developed a fine reputation as a deluxe, long-distance cruise ship – including six weeks around the Mediterranean and two months around Africa. In the end, however, she was reduced to making bargain, pound-a-day voyages. One of her last assignments was to represent Cunard-White Star, along with the *Berengaria*, at King George V's Silver Jubilee Fleet Review off Spithead on 16 July 1935. Cunard's *Lancastria* was also there, but as part of a spectators' cruise out of Liverpool. There had been some talk of steaming-up the otherwise idle *Mauretania* and having her present at the Review as well, but this idea never came to pass.

Two months later, in September 1934, the *Homeric* was laid up (off Ryde on the Isle of Wight). Her cruises were transferred over to the smaller, more efficient *Franconia*. In better financial times, she might have found a buyer, changed hands and continued in service. Instead, in the following year, she was sold for £75,000 ($121,000) to breakers at Inverkeithing. She reached the breakers' yard in March 1935. In all, quite sadly, she had seen only thirteen years of active service.

Arriving in the Hudson River, the 774-foot-long *Homeric* has an imposing appearance. (Cunard)

Above: Another view of a busy day at Southampton's Ocean Dock – the *Olympic* and *Homeric* are berthed; the *Aquitania* is behind, in dry dock; and bottom, Royal Mail Line's *Araguaya* is berthed. (Author's Collection)

Right: The dome over the First Class main lounge aboard the 2,766-passenger *Homeric* was done in champagne-coloured glass. (Norman Knebel Collection)

Above: The superb smoking room aboard the *Homeric.* (Norman Knebel Collection)

Right: A marble bathroom attached to one of the *Homeric*'s finest suites. (Norman Knebel Collection)

Above: During a Mediterranean cruise, the *Homeric* is anchored off Villefranche on the French Riviera. (Cunard)

Right: Second Class aboard the twin-funnel *Homeric*. (Norman Knebel Collection)

Pirosc. HOMERIC   EUROPA AMERICA

Seconda Classe

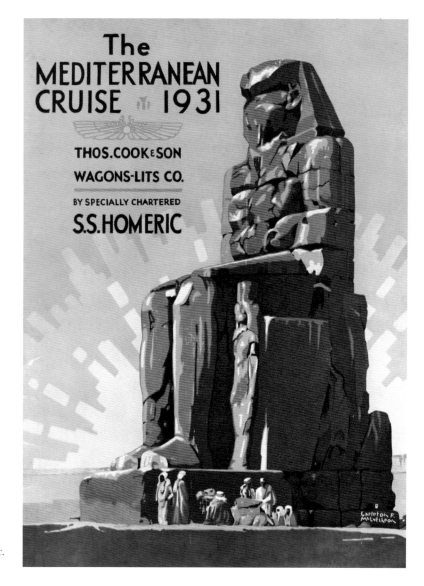

Luxury cruising to the sunny Mediterranean aboard the celebrated *Homeric*.
(Norman Knebel Collection)

Pictorial impressions by Helen Wills

Helen Wills, a passenger on the White Star liner Majestic last summer, illustrated the incidents which impressed her. This is one of a series.

Her comment: " A leisurely sport – shuffleboard. It requires a good eye, true aim and a strong right arm."

Helen Wills

CHOOSE THE SHIP THAT FITS YOUR BUDGET

 For those whose life is set to a speed tempo there are the *Majestic*, world's largest ship, *Olympic, Homeric* and *Belgenland* to England and the Continent. For those who'd enjoy a week at sea, the popular *Minnetonka* and *Minnewaska* direct to London via France. For those who adhere to the modern slogan of "it's smart to be thrifty" there is a fleet of luxurious Cabin liners led by the great new *Britannic*, largest of her kind in the world, with rates from $147.50; and Tourist third cabin accommodations as low as $105—only $120 on two great exclusively "Tourist" ships   Assure yourself an enjoyable crossing and the maximum value for your passage dollar by insisting on booking via White Star, Red Star, or Atlantic Transport Lines.

30 Principal Offices in the U. S. and Canada. Main Office, No. 1 Broadway, New York. Authorized agents everywhere.

WHITE STAR LINE · RED STAR LINE · ATLANTIC TRANSPORT LINE
INTERNATIONAL   MERCANTILE   MARINE   COMPANY

Left: A First Class deck plan aboard the *Homeric*. (Norman Knebel Collection)

Far left: White Star Line crossings – and choosing 'the ship that fits your budget'. The date is 1929. (National Geographic Society)

11. ALBERTIC (1914–20)

A twin-funnel ship of 18,939 tons, the *Albertic* was intended to be a German liner. Laid down in 1914, but with construction halted owing to the war, it was planned that she would be North German Lloyd's *Munchen* and for a secondary, intermediate service between Bremerhaven, Cherbourg, Southampton and New York. Idle and incomplete, she was ceded to the Allies in 1919, finally launched at the AG Weser yard at Bremen on 28 June 1920 and then sold to the Royal Mail Lines. Completion and outfitting was very sluggish, however. It took another three years.

Finally completed as the *Ohio*, she was Royal Mail's largest and fastest ship. The 591-foot-long ship was used on the North Atlantic as intended, sailing between Hamburg, Southampton, Cherbourg and New York, and the occasional voyage between the Mediterranean and New York. She was sold, however, to White Star in the winter of 1927 for £1 million ($287,000). Renamed *Albertic*, she was promptly refitted to suit White Star purposes – for 270 First and 1,100 Tourist Class passengers and assigned to their Liverpool–Quebec City–Montreal service. In early 1929, she was called to other work: replacing the stranded *Celtic* on the Liverpool–Cobh–New York run.

Her operations were varied after the Depression took hold and included a return to Canadian service. Laid up during winter slumps, the *Albertic* was completely laid up, at Holy Loch on the Clyde, by September 1933. She was officially acquired during the Cunard merger in April 1934, but never used. Instead, she was quickly sold for £34,000 for scrapping. In July, she was off to Osaka. The *Albertic* was indeed a sad example of the shortened lives of some Depression-era passenger ships. This otherwise fine little liner sailed for only fourteen years.

12. CALGARIC (1914–21)

The 16,063 grt *Calgaric* was built by Harland & Wolff at Belfast, but not for White Star. Laid down in 1914, work was soon suspended due to the outbreak of war and not resumed for two years. Intended to be a passenger ship, the *Orca*, for the Pacific Steam Navigation Company Co. Ltd, she was – owing to a pressing post-war need – finished as a cargo ship. In 1921, however, she returned to her builders' yard and was outfitted as a passenger ship, carrying 190 First, 220 Second and 480 Third Class passengers, intended for Pacific Steam's usual Liverpool–west coast of South America service, but instead reassigned upon completion to Royal Mail Lines for their North Atlantic trade. She was assigned to their Hamburg–Southampton–New York service, usually with a westbound call at Halifax. But after Royal Mail withdrew from North Atlantic service in December 1926, she was transferred, within Royal Mail's ownership of White Star, to the latter company for its Canadian service. Refitted for 290 First, 550 Tourist and 330 Third Class passengers, the ship was renamed *Calgaric* in the winter of 1927 and assigned to the Liverpool–Quebec City–Montreal run with cruising in the winter months.

Affected rather quickly by the downturns of the Depression, the 550-foot-long *Calgaric* was laid up – but kept in 'sea ready' status – at Milford Haven in Wales. She returned, although quite briefly, in the summer of 1931. Afterwards, she was idle for two years before returning briefly to the Canadian run in the summer of 1933.

By 1933, White Star ships were often much less than even half-full. The *Majestic* arrived in New York, for example, on a winter crossing with a mere 200 passengers onboard. The company's losses amounted to £353,552 for the year ($96,000). In the summer of 1933, ships such as the smallish but struggling *Calgaric* had something of an added reprieve: a special charter cruise – to the Boy Scouts and Girl Guides Association. The party was not large, however, consisting of 100 Scouts, 475 Guides and 80 attendants. Lord and Lady Baden-Powell, the Chief Scout and Chief Guide, were aboard. The cruise visited the Baltic and Oslo and returned via the north of Scotland to Liverpool. Soon afterward, she was again laid-up at Milford Haven.

There was little hope with Cunard-White Star's new combined fleet for the *Calgaric*. She was sold in December 1934 for £31,000 to breakers at Pembroke. Rather poetically, she reached the scrappers' yard on Christmas Day.

13. MAJESTIC (1922)

Perhaps my favourite model in that vestibule gallery at Cunard's long-ago headquarters at 25 Broadway was the *Majestic*. It too was superbly created by Basset Lowke and measured 18 feet in length. The great masts seem to tower higher than usual, for example, the three funnels had their graceful slant and what seemed to be dozens of lifeboats were tucked everywhere. The rigging was perfect, the brass propellers shining and every detail, including passenger benches on deck, added to this fantasy-like creation. I would stare longer at that model of the *Majestic* than any other in that Cunard collection of some fifty years ago. When Cunard left 25 Broadway, the company's opulent Lower Manhattan headquarters, and moved uptown, to Park Avenue, in 1968. The model of the *Majestic* was given to the then brand-new South Street Seaport Museum, also in Lower Manhattan. The museum was more informal in its early years and, most unfortunately, the model of the *Majestic* disappeared. Presumed stolen, it has never been seen again.

The impressive, three-funnel *Majestic* – affectionately dubbed the 'Magic Stick' by fond passengers, crew and even the local dockers and tugboat crews at New York and Southampton – was the premier ship in the White Star fleet at the time of the merger in 1934. She was still the world's largest liner – 56,551 gross tons and 956 feet in length – a prized distinction that she held from 1922 until the advent, in spring 1935, of the 79,000 grt, 1,028-foot-long French *Normandie*.

The *Majestic* was the third of Hamburg America Line's pre-First World War superliners. The earlier ships were the 52,000-ton *Imperator*, which became Cunard's *Berengaria*, and, slightly larger, the 54,000-ton *Vaterland*, which became the American *Leviathan*. The *Majestic* was first named *Bismarck*, but never sailed for the Germans on the North Atlantic run to New York and sat out the war years idle and incomplete. There were rumours that, when completed, the *Bismarck* – as the world's largest ship and pride of the German fleet – was to take the Kaiser on an around-the-world victory cruise. Instead, the Germans lost the war, the Kaiser was in exile by 1919 and the *Bismarck* was passed to an Allied reparations committee for disposal. She finally passed to White Star, in compensation for the German sinking of the *Britannic*. After completion work and outfitting at Hamburg (supervised by Harland & Wolff), she was commissioned under the British flag and as the White Star flagship in the spring of 1922. She had a serious fire in 1920, which delayed her delivery and which was suspected to be sabotage. The Germans were resentful about surrendering the ship.

Quickly, she entered commercial service and, quite soon, was accorded a special honour: a visit at Southampton by King George V and Queen Mary. The *Majestic* was teamed, on the Southampton–Cherbourg–New York run, with the *Olympic* and the *Homeric*. She was fitted out to carry as many as 2,145 passengers – 750 First Class, 545 Second Class, 850 Third Class. In 1923, she once crossed with 2,625 passengers onboard, the greatest number in White Star history. The *Majestic* also had great speed. During a crossing in September 1923, she averaged almost 25 knots. Only surpassed by the *Mauretania*, she was said to be the second-fastest Atlantic liner.

The *Majestic* was very popular in the twenties. White Star promotional literature stated that her interiors were so large and spacious that they were altogether equivalent to 400 eight-room houses. The columned indoor pool, done in Pompeian style, had a full depth of almost 10 feet. The domed-ceiling dining room, surely one of the largest of its kind at sea in the 1920s, could accommodate almost 700 at one sitting. The superb main lounge was described as: 'Lofty, spacious, dignified, the *Majestic*'s lounge is distinguished by perfect symmetry, by substantial beauty of its oak-panelled walls with hand-carved ornamentation, by its tall French windows and by the richness of the ceiling of crystal and carved wood.'

Structurally, the *Majestic* developed a mid-ships crack in her hull. Thereafter, the plating on both sides was strengthened. The ship was always 'suspect', however, for White Star engineers. During her career, the *Majestic* also encountered several fierce Atlantic storms. In September 1934, she was slammed by such a huge North Atlantic wave that tons of water all but flooded her upper decks, the bridge windows were smashed and her master was so injured that the staff captain had to assume command. The captain was in hospital for a month and never sailed again.

On 26 July 1934, King George V and Queen Mary opened the new graving dock at Southampton. Named the King George V Graving Dock, the 'KG5' to locals, the first ship to use it was aptly the world's largest, the *Majestic*. The ship's arrival created a tremendous spectacle: the world's biggest liner and one of the world's biggest docks. The dock was purposely created for even bigger liners, the *Queen Mary*, due in 1936, and the *Queen Elizabeth* beginning in 1940.

In 1934, there were more serious problems: too few passengers. The likes of the half-empty *Majestic*, often seen scarred with rust and looking somewhat faded, struggled. The new Cunard-White Star firm moved quickly – almost all White Star tonnage would be disposed of. The obvious exceptions were the two newest ships, the *Britannic* of 1930 and the *Georgic* of 1932. But on the disposal list were the *Adriatic*, *Albertic*, *Homeric*, *Olympic*, *Doric* and *Calgaric*. Another ship, the *Laurentic*, was chartered out for peacetime trooping and then laid up.

The *Majestic* was retired in February 1936 and laid up along the Southampton Docks awaiting sale. Less than three months later and after only fourteen years of active service, she was sold to breakers in Scotland for £115,000. She was to be broken up at Rosyth. In preparation, her three funnels and twin masts were trimmed so as to ensure clear passage under the Forth railway bridge. Then, quite suddenly, her fate seemed to change: the British Admiralty needed her as a moored training centre for 2,000 young naval cadets. Conveniently, she would be berthed at Rosyth, a Royal Navy base. She was actually obtained in a trade: the Admiralty gave twenty-four old warships (equivalent to the 56,000 tons of the liner) to the shipbreakers in return for the *Majestic*, which was commissioned as HMS *Caledonia*. She was, in fact, listed – amid mighty battleships – as the largest ship in active service.

After war was declared on 3 September 1939, immediate precautions included evacuating all cadets and staff from the *Caledonia*. The Royal Navy was already worried about possible Nazi air attacks in or near Rosyth. Even the ship itself was considered a possible target. Being powerless (her engines had been removed), she was shifted from the main shipping area and then beached elsewhere. There must have been some thought, however, of re-engining the ship and reactivating her as a much-needed troopship. This never came to pass. All but empty, she caught fire on 29 September and burned out beyond repair. Her remains were re-sold to the scrappers, but dismantling was sluggish. The hull was not fully demolished for four years, until 1943, at Inverkeithing.

As the war started in that fateful late summer of 1939, all of the great and grand floating palaces except the *Aquitania* were gone. The *Mauretania*, *Berengaria*, *Olympic*, *Homeric* and even America's *Leviathan* were gone, each broken up. The *Majestic* would soon be destroyed as well. In retrospect, if these aged liners had been kept in reserve, they might have been restored and put to good use as important troop ships. By 1939, the age of the floating palaces was over; three-liner express services on the Atlantic and the great heyday of the White Star Line were finished.

Above: The mighty, 950-foot-long *Majestic* is carefully positioned into the big graving dock at the Boston Naval Shipyard. (Cronican-Arroyo Collection)

Right: A busy day along the Chelsea Piers in 1934: from top to bottom – the *Manhattan, Georgic, Majestic, Leviathan, Pennland* and *Paris*. (Author's Collection)

Above: Night-time work: the *Majestic* in the huge floating dock at Southampton. (Cunard)

Right: Splendour at sea – (top) the oak-panelled entrance of the main lounge and (bottom) the main lounge with a ceiling of carved wood and gleaming crystal. (Norman Knebel Collection)

Left: Fitness at sea: four times around the enclosed promenade deck aboard the *Majestic* equalled 1 mile. (Norman Knebel Collection)

Far left: The First Class dining room (top) and the starboard side of the same room (bottom). (Norman Knebel Collection)

Above: Another celebrity passenger aboard White Star: Lord Inchcape arriving in New York aboard the *Majestic* on 16 May 1922. (Author's Collection)

Right: A *Majestic* booklet cover, dated 1922. (Norman Knebel Collection)

MAJESTIC

WHITE ★ STAR ★ LINE
NEW YORK

THE WORLD'S LARGEST SHIP

Above: With her masts and funnels cut down, the *Majestic* is taking a turn in the King George V Graving Dock at Southampton before heading off to the scrappers in Scotland. (Cunard)

Left: Winter cruises in 1931 included a five-night voyage aboard the *Majestic*. Fares began at $60 or $12 per person per day. (National Geographic Society)

14. DORIC (1923)

Built at Belfast, the 16,484 grt *Doric* was one of a series of similar passenger liners built in the early twenties. The 601-foot-long ship was designed purposely for White Star's Liverpool–Eastern Canada service, carrying as many as 2,300 passengers – 600 Cabin Class and 1,700 Third. A conservative ship, she was rather dated upon completion in May 1923 – she was coal-fired. Later, she alternated her crossings with some winter cruising and, by the early 1930s, was used far more for cruising.

White Star certainly had its share of problems in 1935. Two weeks after the *Laurentic* was involved in a serious collision in the Irish Sea, the *Doric* was involved in a more serious one. On 5 September, while on a pound-a-day Mediterranean cruise from Southampton, the *Doric* was in collision with the French vessel *Formigny* of Chargeurs Réunis off the coast of Spain. For the White Star liner, there were serious damages, including the flooding of a forward hold, a list and, with a fear of sinking, she finally requested assistance. A nearby P&O liner, the *Viceroy of India*, took on 241 of the *Doric*'s passengers; the *Orion* of the Orient Line later took on 486 passengers and forty-two crew. All passengers were returned to the UK. The limping *Doric* later put into Vigo for emergency repairs. Afterward, she returned to England. While she was only twelve years old, full repairs would have been costly compared to the still weak financial position of the combined Cunard-White Star operations. Without much hesitancy, it would seem, the *Doric* was sold for as little as £35,000 to shipbreakers. She was promptly delivered at Newport in Monmouthshire and demolished. Some of her fittings and furnishings, dining room chairs, lounge sofas and ceiling lamps, were sold at auction to raise extra monies.

Dressed in the flags for another cruise, the *Doric* had a comparatively very short career. (Alex Duncan)

15. *LAURENTIC* (1927)

Philip King's father worked for White Star, beginning as a bellboy in 1934 aboard the *Laurentic*. He recalled:

> My father was then just fifteen and he earned one pound a week or about $3. Bellboys did all sorts of jobs – including polishing the silver and waxing the leaves on the fern plants in the lobby. It was all very strict, very punctual, almost military-like in its rules and day-to-day life was hardly comfortable. My father told me he slept down on the lowest deck in a cabin with about fifteen other boys and young deckhands. He stayed with the sea, moving to the new *Queen Mary* in 1937, and was still with Cunard when the war started in September 1939.

The *Laurentic*, at 18,724 tons and 600 feet in length, was a bit of a misfit. She was, quite oddly, finished as a coal burner as late as the autumn of 1927. She had dated triple-expansion engines as well as more austere quarters than other White Star liners of the time. Used on the Liverpool–Quebec City–Montreal service, she had suitable three class quarters – 594 Cabin Class, 406 Tourist and 500 Third. Her crew numbered 420.

The *Laurentic* not only did her share of cruises, but charters as well. In March 1934, she was off on a Roman Catholic pilgrimage, sailing from Dublin to Naples (for Rome) with 700 pilgrims. Ten altars were especially fitted onboard and a cinema added to the ship's amenities.

On 18 August 1935, while outbound from Liverpool on a Northern Cities cruise with 620 passengers aboard, the *Laurentic* collided with a Blue Star Line freighter, the *Napier Star*. The incident occurred in the Irish Sea in thick fog. Six members of the *Napier Star*'s crew were killed and four injured. The Blue Star ship tore a great hole in the starboard bow of the *Laurentic*, smashing twelve crew cabins in the bow section. While passengers took to their muster stations, there was no danger and no injuries on the White Star liner. She did, however, return to Liverpool and her passengers were transferred to cruises aboard the *Homeric* and *Lancastria*. In subsequent court inquiries, both the *Laurentic* and *Napier Star* were found to be at fault.

By December 1935, with only eight years of passenger service on her record, the *Laurentic* was laid up. Her commercial passenger days were over. She was revived in September 1936, but only for a charter to the

British Government. She would carry troops but only on one voyage to Palestine. 1935 was, however, an encouraging year. Cunard-White Star carried over 134,000 Atlantic passengers – twice the number of such competitors as the Hamburg America Line or North German Lloyd.

The *Laurentic* was laid-up once again, beginning in January 1937, first in Southampton Water and then at Dartmouth on the River Dart.

She was quickly reactivated for war duties during a refit at Plymouth in September 1939. Her role: armed merchant cruiser. While she grounded in fog on Islay in January 1940 and needed six weeks of repairs afterward, her end was not far off – she was torpedoed three times by a German U-boat while assisting a stricken ship on 3 November.

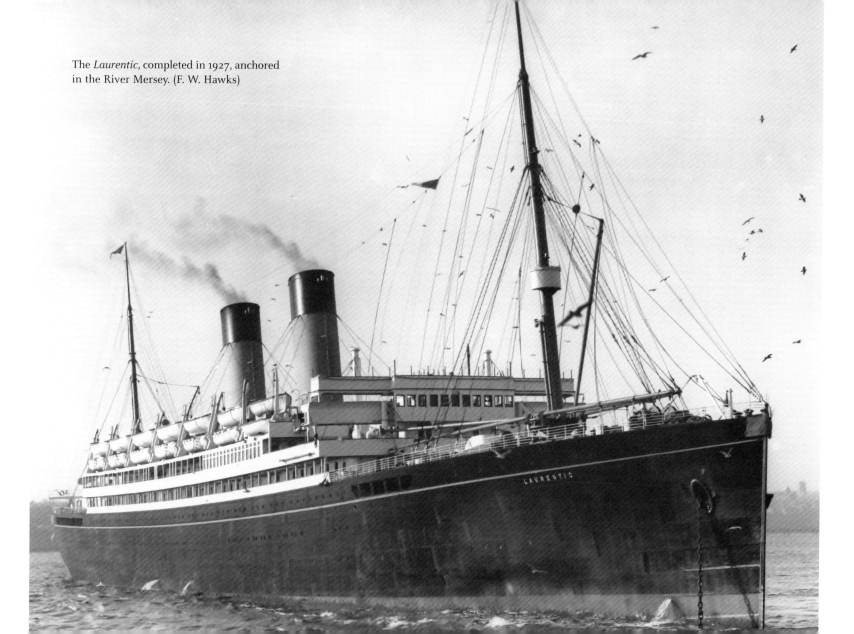

The *Laurentic*, completed in 1927, anchored in the River Mersey. (F. W. Hawks)

16. BRITANNIC (1930)

Some ships, as I recall seeing them, had an added elegance, something different when seeing them underway. Often on Friday afternoons, after the school week finished, I'd hurry over to the Hoboken waterfront to watch the late afternoon departures. A regular in the 1950s was Cunard's *Britannic*. Very often, she'd depart at 3.30 p.m. from her usual berth, the north side of Pier 92. She'd have a fast and efficient and very timely undocking, and would be passing Hoboken, about 2 miles downriver, by 4 p.m. With her squat, slightly raked funnels and two tall masts, she seemed to race by – and with that elegance. The *Queen Mary* and *Queen Elizabeth* always looked more dramatic, more imposing and certainly big and powerful as they slipped by. The *Britannic* was more graceful, even purposeful and much like, say, a well trained ballerina. Two other occasions come to mind of this last of the White Star liners. Once, during a late morning departure (usually at 11.30 a.m. from Pier 92), she came down along the Hudson in a thick fog. Slowly, her silhouette appeared. The view remained in the grey of the fog; it was not detailed, but included a sudden screech on her steam whistle. A tug and barge were in her path and, being bigger,

had to move. On another day, a chilly, grey November afternoon, and with the daylight giving way to night soon after 4 p.m., the *Britannic* was arriving, assisted by a team of Moran tugs. She was proceeding slowly, no doubt arriving late, and was moving along the Hudson at a slow speed. The port had that quiet Saturday afternoon mood – fewer ships, only the odd tug and barge underway, the shipyards silent and altogether the mood broken only by the inbound *Britannic*. In the great collection of liners that visited New York in the 1950s, the *Britannic* was to me a very special ship.

Motor liners came into vogue on the North Atlantic. By 1925, there were the likes of Sweden's 17,900 grt *Gripsholm* and, far larger, Italy's 32,600 grt *Augustus* three years later. Diesels were said to be not only more efficient, but supposedly created a smoother sailing. This appealed to ship owners, particularly passenger ship lines, and White Star was among them. Furthermore, after leaving J. P. Morgan's ownership in the mid-1920s, White Star joined a consortium known as the Royal Mail Group. Their management strongly preferred motor liners. Overall on the Atlantic, there was also a growing interest in so-called 'cabin liners', ships that offered Cabin Class accommodation instead of First Class as their premium space. This meant greater comfort and luxury, but at Cabin Class fares. Generally and in the troubled days of the thirties, it was yet another strategy to lure more passengers.

Rather oddly, in 1927, White Star added the 19,000-ton *Laurentic*, which was very dated in design. Not only did she have pre-First World War-style triple-expansion engines, but she ranked as the Atlantic's last newly built coal burner. But within a year, in 1928, White Star changed course completely – the company planned a new liner that would use diesels and which would rank as one of the most economical liners of her day, thoughtfully using far less fuel oil.

The 26,943 grt *Britannic* even looked modern. She had the long, low, almost very lean look of a 'thirties motor liner'. Her funnels were low, slightly raked, almost stumped. The forward one was, in fact, a dummy and included the 712-foot-long ship's wireless room. Her whistles were unusually fixed on the second funnel and on the forward mast. There was one rather old-fashioned touch: the use of quadrant davits for her lifeboats. By the late twenties, gravity davits were very much in use. Those quadrant davits remained aboard the 18-knot, twin-screw *Britannic* to the very end of her days.

As built, at White Star's favourite shipyard, Harland & Wolff at Belfast, the *Britannic* carried 1,553 passengers – 504 Cabin Class, 551 Tourist Class and 498 Third Class. In 1939, a Cabin Class stateroom was priced at $244 on a peak, summer season, eight-night crossing between New York and London.

The *Britannic*'s interiors were very much 'British ocean liner deco', using lighter woods, inlaid wood floors, burl wood columns, chromium-encased lighting fixtures and carpets with swirls and other dramatic patterns. Among her cabins, most Cabin Class staterooms had private bathroom facilities. After the Second World War, when the *Britannic* was refurbished following troopship duties, furnishings and carpets from the *Aquitania* were taken from storage. They were placed aboard the renewed *Britannic*.

When she reappeared at New York in May 1948, the *Britannic* had been altered. Her capacity had been greatly reduced – from 1,553 to 993 (429 in First Class and 564 in Tourist). She and her near-sister *Georgic* were the only survivors of the pre-war White Star fleet; the *Britannic* was the only one to be fully restored for luxury service. Cunard marketed her as 'the brilliant *Britannic*' and she soon had a reputation for a certain 'clubbiness' on her monthly sailings between New York, Cobh and Liverpool. She was teamed with the 250-passenger, all-First Class combination passenger-cargo ships *Media* and *Parthia*.

Each winter in the 1950s, and although she lacked spacious lido decks and outdoor pools and was without air-conditioning, the *Britannic* – with her capacity reduced to a more intimate 400 – set off from New York each January on a nine-week Mediterranean cruise. Her itinerary on her final Mediterranean–Black Sea cruise, which began in January 1960, included Madeira, Casablanca, Tangier, Malta, Alexandria, Haifa, Larnaca, Rhodes, Istanbul, the Dardanelles, Piraeus, Dubrovnik, Venice, Messina, Naples, Villefranche, Barcelona, Palma, Algiers, Málaga, Gibraltar, Lisbon, Cherbourg and finally Southampton, where the cruise ended. Minimum fare was $1,275 and included First Class return to New York within twelve months on any Cunard liner including the *Queen Mary* and *Queen Elizabeth*.

Although the Cunard-White Star name had been dropped after 1950, Cunard managers allowed the *Britannic* to retain her original White Star black-and-buff funnels to the end of her days, in December 1960. Her final year was marred in fact by mechanical troubles, a broken

crankshaft, which kept her idle along the south side of Pier 90 for most of the prime summer season. Repairs then ranked as the most thorough and extensive done at a berth rather than an actual shipyard. But the *Britannic*'s days were clearly numbered – on a dark, cold November afternoon, she departed from New York on her final crossing to Liverpool. After being de-stored, she sailed from Liverpool and headed for the shipbreakers at Inverkeithing.

Above: Artist John Lee's depiction of the *Britannic* arriving at New York. (John Lee)

Left: Outbound from New York on a long, winter Mediterranean cruise, the 712-foot-long *Britannic* was the last of the White Star liners. (Cunard)

Above: With her funnels already painted in black as a disguise following the start of the Second World War, the *Britannic* is seen in the Mersey in September 1939. (Cronican-Arroyo Collection)

Right: During a New York dockers' strike, the *Britannic* joins the re-routed *Queen Elizabeth* at Halifax in this view from the winter of 1955. (Halifax Maritime Museum)

Cunard Line

M.V. "Britannic"

GROSS TONNAGE 27,666

PLAN OF FIRST CLASS ACCOMMODATION

This Christmas..

"THE WORLD AND ALL ITS WONDERS!"

A GIFT from the gods—a winter cruise to thrilling, exotic lands sunny southern skies—why not take the whole family this winter? It's the finest Christmas gift in all the world—a gift of health and pleasure. And this year, at rates to fit every purse—it's a *real investment!*

WINTER CRUISES FOR EVERYONE

Planned to modern conditions—*complete*, yet short enough not to keep you away too long—and moderately priced in keeping with present day economy. In every case the ship is your hotel throughout—at no extra cost.

MEDITERRANEAN

BRITANNIC (England's largest motor ship) **Sails Jan. 9**

HOMERIC (Ship of Splendor) **Sails Jan. 22, Feb. 22**

28-30 DAYS—$475 (up) First Class $245 Tourist

Short cruises—yet complete. So expertly arranged that you really see the high spots of the Mediterranean—not just three or four brief stops—but an itinerary including Las Palmas (Canary Islands), Casablanca and Rabat, Gibraltar, Algiers, Palermo, Naples and Pompeii, Monte Carlo and Nice, Barcelona and Madeira.

WEST INDIES

Here's the most comprehensive list of West Indies trips offered. No matter when you want to go or how much time you can spare we have *your* cruise.

12-day "High Spot" Cruises to Havana, Nassau, Bermuda.
M. V. *Britannic*, sailing Dec. 26 (New Year's Eve and Day in Havana).
S. S. *Lapland*, sailing Jan. 7, Jan. 21, Feb. 4, Feb. 18, Mar. 3 and Mar. 17

15-16-day Caribbean Cruises including Panama Canal.
S. S. *Belgenland*, Jan. 20, Feb. 6, 24.—M. V. *Britannic*, Feb. 10, 26, Mar. 15.

10-day Triangle Cruises to Havana, and Nassau or Bermuda.
S. S. *Belgenland*, Mar. 12, Mar. 23*, Apr. 5—S. S. *Homeric*, Mar. 24, Apr. 6.
*Havana, Nassau *and* Bermuda.

Let us, or our authorized travel agents in your community give you the full details regarding the cruise or cruises in which you are interested. It will be good news.

WHITE STAR LINE   RED STAR LINE
INTERNATIONAL MERCANTILE MARINE COMPANY
No. 1 Broadway, N. Y; 180 N. Michigan Ave., Chicago, 687 Market St., San Francisco; our offices elsewhere or any authorized steamship agent.

Left: Cruising in the winter of 1931/32, which includes voyages on the then brand-new *Britannic*. (National Geographic Society)

Far left: Post-war: a First Class deck plan of the *Britannic*. (Norman Knebel Collection)

Opposite left: Eight-day voyages to Nassau and Havana aboard the 26,943 grt *Britannic* and her near-sister, the *Georgic*. (Norman Knebel Collection)

Opposite right: Summer escapes in 1934 aboard White Star's two newest liners. (Norman Knebel Collection)

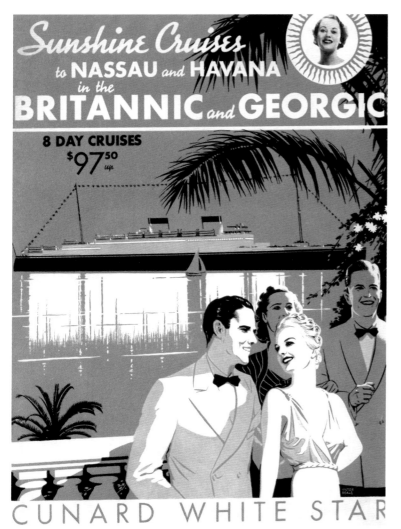

Left: Each winter in the 1950s, the *Britannic* went off on a two-month-long Mediterranean cruise. (Norman Knebel Collection)

Far left: During cruises, the *Britannic* as well as the *Georgic* carried approximately 600 all-First Class passengers. (Norman Knebel Collection)

Above: Post-war travel between Liverpool, Cobh and New York: the First Class main lounge aboard the *Britannic*. (Norman Knebel Collection)

Right: The *Britannic's* First Class long gallery (top) and the First Class cocktail lounge (bottom). (Norman Knebel Collection)

Above: The *Britannic* passes the outbound *Media* in the Hudson River. (Author's Collection)

Right: When she was retired in late 1960, the *Britannic* was the last survivor of the White Star fleet. (Cronican-Arroyo Collection)

17. GEORGIC (1932)

Although long gone, having been merged into a huge banking consortium, New York City's Seamen's Bank was well known for the glass-cased ship models used to dress up the lobbies of its many branches. Mostly, however, they were sailing ships, vessels of the eighteenth and nineteenth centuries. One, as I recall from the 1960s, was an exception. In its branch on West 23rd Street and along Tenth Avenue, the main window contained a 10-foot-long model of Cunard-White Star's *Georgic*. It had obviously been a gift from the ship's owners, possibly from just after the Second World War. The model sat in well-lighted perfection and, I am sure, sparked great interest. These days, that branch office is long since gone and the whereabouts of that splendid model are unknown. A sister-model of the *Britannic* was thirty or so city streets north, in a shop window along Twelfth Avenue and quite close to the famed ocean liner piers, 'Luxury Liner Row' as it was known. When the shop closed in the 1970s, the model found its way into private hands, however, then passed through a maritime auction in 2010 and is now in other ownership.

The earlier *Britannic* had initially been ordered alone, but after the cancellation of the far larger *Oceanic* in the summer of 1929, a second liner, a near-sister, was ordered. Completed in June 1932, the 27,759 grt *Georgic* was slightly larger and also included some different design touches such as having a rounded forward superstructure (rather than squared, as aboard the *Britannic*). The 711-foot-long *Georgic* was in fact the last White Star liner to be built and therefore the end of their association with a long-time friend: Harland & Wolff Limited at Belfast.

Even in the otherwise hard-pressed 1930s, the *Britannic* and the *Georgic* were very popular ships. In 1933, in fact, the *Britannic* carried more passengers than any other liner in the White Star fleet. In June 1933, the *Britannic* carried 1,103 passengers during one crossing, the highest amount for any Atlantic liner that year. Both had fine accommodations, even in lower-deck Third Class. One-way in a Third Class four-berth cabin cost £19 (or $55) in 1935. Both ships also did considerable cruising: $100 for eight days to Bermuda and Nassau from New York in the late 1930s; $210 for eighteen days to the Caribbean; and $660 for forty-two days to the Mediterranean.

When the Second World War began, both the *Britannic* and *Georgic* were converted for trooping. The *Georgic* was very nearly an early casualty. On 14 July 1941, she was moored at Egypt's Port Tewfik during a Nazi air raid. She was bombed and promptly caught fire. Then there were further problems: her fans and blowers spread the blaze through the ship's interior. In the end, as the fire diminished, the *Georgic* was a badly burned and blistered ship. Few thought she could be saved. But because of the urgencies of war and especially the need for large troopships, she was temporarily repaired and patched and then towed by two freighters to Port Sudan. Further repair work was slow, however. She was moved to Karachi in March 1942 and, by December, towed to Bombay. Later, in a long, very careful process, she was towed round the South African Cape, along the eastern Atlantic and taken in hand by Harland & Wolff at Belfast for full repairs and, even if much reduced, modification. She returned to trooping service in December 1944, having missed over three years of use, but as a much changed ship. With twisted beams and mangled steel panels, she was no longer a Cunard-White Star luxury liner. Even her passage ways were uneven and, by crew and passengers alike, she was dubbed 'the corrugated lung'.

From 1949 through 1955, the *Britannic*'s greatly rebuilt near-sister *Georgic* – then owned by the British Ministry of Transport – was under charter to Cunard but only for peak summer season crossings. Carrying up to 1,962 all-Tourist Class passengers, she was a budget ship providing low-fare service for tourists, students and migrants. She was very much a demoded ship, even below regular Tourist Class on other Cunarders, had one less funnel and, because of structural problems, was not allowed to sail the North Atlantic in winter. For Cunard, she usually sailed between Liverpool or Southampton, Le Havre, Cobh, Halifax and New York. In the winter, off-season months, the *Georgic* sailed mostly to Australia and New Zealand with outward migrants and bargain tourists on the homeward voyages. She also carried Dutch colonial evacuees from troubled Indonesia, troops in the Korean War and groups of British military forces and their families from colonial outposts such as Hong Kong and Singapore.

Aged twenty-four, the *Georgic* was retired in December 1955 and soon sent off to scrappers at Faslane.

Opposite left: Cheering crowds: it is July 1939 and the *Georgic* sails off from New York's Pier 56. (Cronican-Arroyo Collection)

Opposite right: Sunshine: two long Caribbean cruises aboard the *Georgic*. (Norman Knebel Collection)

Demoded: after the war, the *Georgic* reappeared with a single stack and single mast. (Cunard)

18. QUEEN MARY (1936)

The World Ship Society's Port of New York Branch began in late 1965. Membership grew quickly, monthly meetings were organized and, on occasion, there were special outings. One of the first was the charter of a Circle Line sightseeing craft for a very special, if sad, occasion: the final sailing from New York of the beloved *Queen Mary*. Under late summer skies with bright sunshine offset with silvery clouds, we stood in position – along with an armada of tugs, fireboats, pleasure craft and other excursion vessels – as the last of the three-stackers departed from the south side of Pier 92. Dressed in flags and with her mighty whistles sounding often, the grand ship looked majestic, regal, every inch the great liner. We followed the ship as she steamed slowly down along the Hudson, into the Lower Bay and then out under the Verrazano-Narrows Bridge. It was goodbye not only to a splendid ship, but in ways to an entire era. The age of many trans-Atlantic liners was drawing quickly to a close. The *Queen Mary*'s final departure was, in many ways, a curtain closing.

It is a well-told, almost classic story – the new Cunard superliner was to be named *Victoria*, keeping the traditional 'ia' ending for a Cunard naming. When the time came (in 1934) to inform King George V of this decision to use his grandmother's name, Sir Ashley Sparkes, Cunard's top executive in North America, requested an audience at Buckingham Palace. He said: 'Your Majesty, we are pleased to inform you that Cunard wishes your approval to name our newest and greatest liner after England's greatest queen.' Without much hesitation, the king replied: 'My wife would be delighted!' His wife was of course Queen Mary. The name of the new Cunard superliner was changed forthwith.

In the late twenties, before the Wall Street Crash, Cunard was enthusiastic about the future of trans-Atlantic trade. It was also the renewed age of the superliner – the Germans were just adding their *Bremen* and *Europa*, both of which would surpass the long-lasting speed record of Cunard's *Mauretania*. Even Canadian Pacific was building their biggest liner yet, the 42,000-ton *Empress of Britain*. White Star was going steps further, planning for a 60,000-tonner to be named *Oceanic*. Furthermore, the Italians were planning two superliners, even if for Mediterranean–New York service, and then, most serious of all, the French had a 75,000-tonner on their drawing boards. It was, in retrospect, a dazzling era – bigger and bigger ships, faster ones and more luxurious liners as well.

John Brown & Company Limited, a long-time favourite of Cunard's, was given the order to build the new company flagship. The first keel plates were laid down two days after Christmas in 1930. The design plans showed not only a very large ship (the world's largest, in fact), but a very powerful one as well (hopefully making it the fastest ship afloat). Could Cunard be considering another Blue Riband champion? The initial answer from their palatial Liverpool headquarters was an emphatic 'no'.

Rather interestingly, Cunard had not built a superliner in some fifteen years, since the *Aquitania* of 1914. That older ship's blueprints were brought out in fact, used and supported the Cunard company's otherwise rather conservative theory that Atlantic liners, even big ones, should appear sturdy, dependable and reliable. Cunard did not follow the more innovative, even futuristic, approach of the rival French Line. The new Cunarder would not only look solid, but would be traditional and unpretentious.

The disruptive effects of the Depression reached Cunard as well as the Clyde in 1931, however. The construction of the new liner was stopped a full year after beginning, in December. Well over 3,000 workers were laid off; a mere fifty were kept on as engineers and watchmen. The great hull just sat – silent, lonesome, rusting and a nesting site for local birds. There were debates in Liverpool but also in London over the ship's future. Should the project be abandoned and the existing hull scrapped? Some thought the new liner was misguided and even wasteful – and, after all, geared mostly to the American travelling public. Fortunately, a positive approach was taken in the end. The British Government loaned Cunard the monies needed to continue – and build an equally large running-mate – so that, after two and a half years, construction restarted. Had it not been for this delay, the new liner would have been in Atlantic service well before her French rival. As it was, the French supership, the *Normandie*, took the early glories. She was the first liner to exceed 1,000 feet in length, the first to exceed 60,000 tons and – far worse in Cunard's thinking – captured the much-prized Blue Riband. The Cunard flagship could only have latter glory.

Her Majesty Queen Mary had consented to name the liner. It would be the first merchant ship so honoured by a reigning monarch. In any event, the public first heard of the name choice on 26 September 1934. Both the king and queen travelled to the John Brown yards at Clydebank for the naming and launching before 100,000 spectators. The event was broadcast on the radio and, throughout the Empire, listeners heard the queen's twenty-eight-word speech and afterward the roar and rumble of the ship's sliding into the River Clyde. A great day for Cunard, it was also a great day for Britain itself. In the grim days of the Depression, the construction of a stunning luxury ship was seen as a bright, very positive light. The queen used a bottle of Australian wine for the naming and later recorded in her diary: 'A most impressive sight but unfortunately it rained all day.'

The 1,018-foot-long hull of the *Queen Mary* was quickly moved to a fitting-out berth. The all but complete ship left the Clyde eighteen months later, on 26 March 1936. A slow, careful progress, it took 4 hours for her to sail along the Clyde and reach the Gare Loch. On 25 May, Queen Mary and her son, the future King Edward VIII, along with other members of the royal family visited the new Cunarder at Southampton. A day later, the 80,774 grt liner set sail on her first voyage to New York. Cunard publicists released endless streams of facts and details. The 140-ton rudder had a door in its side so that it could be inspected internally in dry dock. There were two 16-ton anchors, each with 990 feet of anchor chain. The ship had 151 watertight compartments, 10,000,000 rivets, 2,000 portholes and windows, 2,500 square feet of glass and 257,000 turbine blades. Each of the three thunderous whistles weighed 1 ton and, when sounded, could be heard for 10 miles. There were 700 clocks and 600 phones onboard. Especially intriguing were the comparisons. If standing on end, the *Queen*

Mary would be taller than the Eiffel Tower, almost as tall as the Empire State Building and would dwarf Big Ben in London. Another exemplified Cunard's great growth: the company's entire fleet totalled 81,000 tons in 1876 and it was 81,000 tons for a single liner half a century later.

The steam turbine, quadruple-screw *Queen Mary* excelled from day one. She made worldwide headlines when, in less than three months, she captured the Blue Riband, outstepping the *Normandie* with a speed of 30.63 knots. The Riband went back to the French flagship in March 1937, only to be regained permanently by the Cunarder in August 1938. Her best record speed was 31.6 knots. The *Queen Mary* remained the world's fastest liner until the maiden voyage of the *United States* in July 1952.

The *Queen Mary* as built could carry 2,139 passengers – 776 Cabin Class, 784 Tourist and 579 Third. Fares in 1938 for her high season, summertime five-night crossings between New York, Cherbourg and Southampton were posted at $282 in Cabin Class (the equivalent of First Class), $149 in Tourist and $93 Third Class. She almost immediately established herself as a beloved ship, preferred by passengers and crew alike, because of an almost undefinable charm of fine service, her handpicked, all-British staff and an onboard warmth and charm. 'It was as if something was in the wood panels,' said a former waiter. 'The *Queen Mary* had this great charm, almost like no other ship, and it embraced you. Passengers and crew alike preferred, even loved the *Mary*!' Onboard, she was classic ocean liner art deco: swirl carpets and lino flooring, polished woods and crystal glass lamps, oversized chairs and deeply cushioned sofas. Although the *Queen Mary* lacked the glitter, high fascination and the pretention of the *Normandie*, the Cunarder averaged a 98 per cent occupancy factor in her first years. By comparison, in four and a half years of service, the *Normandie* averaged 59 per cent.

The 80,774 grt *Queen Mary* was at sea, en route to New York, when war between Britain and Nazi Germany was declared on 3 September 1939. She was booked over capacity, ferrying home worried tourists and even evacuees. All further crossings for the giant ship were cancelled and, by mid-September, she lost her Cunard colours. She was repainted in sombre grey while lying on the south side of Pier 90 at the foot of West 50th Street. Along with the *Normandie*, *Ile de France* and *Mauretania*, the ship was in a 'holding pattern' – waiting for further developments in the war. Six months later, in March 1940, the *Queen Mary* was joined by her intended fleet-mate, the *Queen Elizabeth*, which had secretly dashed to New York from her birthplace in Scotland for safety. In some six weeks, the *Queen Mary* was gone – making a secret voyage south along the Atlantic, rounding the South African Cape, crossing the Indian Ocean and arriving in Sydney harbour, where she was outfitted for trooping, carrying up to 10,000 soldier-passengers per voyage. The *Elizabeth* would follow in another six months, in November.

At first, both *Queens* operated across the Indian Ocean with Australian troops for Africa. The *Mary* returned to the North Atlantic in the winter of 1942, and began (with the *Elizabeth*) a 'GI shuttle' service between New York and Gourock. Now, she averaged 15,000 service personnel per crossing. In fact, she established the all-time record for any ship when, in July 1943, she crossed with 16,683 onboard. The *Mary* and *Elizabeth* – described as the 'grey ghosts' – were almost beyond attack. Blacked-out and at high speed, they crossed the Atlantic. Beyond the scope of any military escort craft, they sailed alone, in zig-zag fashion and on courses that were not repeated from voyage to voyage. Hitler offered a $250,000 reward to the U-boat commander who could sink one of the Cunard *Queens*. They were the biggest Allied troopships and, by delivering a combined 2.5 million wartime personnel, Churchill himself said the two liners helped reduce the war in Europe by at least a year. A crewmember once told me, 'We were all but run ragged during the war. Voyage after voyage with mostly GI passengers and barely time taken for an overhaul, even short dry dock period.'

There was only one touch of tarnish to the *Queen Mary*'s otherwise golden wartime record. On 2 October 1942, while sailing at top speed off Northern Ireland and en route to Gourock, she rammed and sliced in half the HMS *Curacoa*, an escort cruiser. The warship sank within 3 minutes and all but twenty-six of her 364 crew were lost. Because of the danger of possible lurking Nazi U-boats, the *Mary* sailed off. She was not permitted to stop for any reason in wartime.

The hard-worked *Queen Mary* was decommissioned, finally, in September 1946 and took almost ten months to restore as a luxury liner. She resumed Southampton–Cherbourg–New York sailings on 31 July 1947. Her passenger configuration had changed: 711 First Class, 707 Cabin and 577 Tourist. She joined the *Queen Elizabeth* and thereby created the first two-liner express service in trans-Atlantic history and the most famous and successful pair of liners ever to sail. The *Queens*, almost always fully booked from the start, earned millions for Cunard and, especially with the delivery of the first waves of post-war American tourists, helped restore the post-war British economy. Among the pair, the *Queen Mary* was always the more popular, a great favourite with passengers in all classes and, as a purser once told me, a favourite of the Hollywood set – those film stars that were famously photographed at the ship's rail, in the cathedral-like lounges and in sumptuous suites.

The *Queen Mary* remained very popular until the late 1950s. Then even she began to struggle with competition from a new and different rival: the airlines. Cunard was beginning to think and then re-think its future – and the future of Atlantic liner operations. A three-class replacement for the aging *Mary*, dubbed the *Q3*, was planned in the early 1960s, but then plans were scrapped and reworked as the two-class *Q4* Project, the 65,000 grt, 2,005-passenger *Queen Elizabeth 2*, commissioned in May 1969.

By the mid-1960s, the *Queen Mary* was struggling, aged, grew tired and was less and less competitive. She was sometimes only a third full on her Atlantic crossings and, as alternatives, was sent on five-night cruises between New York and Nassau (with fares from $125) and seven days from Southampton to Las Palmas. It all had changed – both *Queens* were dubbed 'limping leviathans'. The onboard tone changed as well. The British press likened them to faded seaside resorts. One called them 'Cunard-on-sea'. After some three decades of service, the *Queen Mary* was hardly a suitable cruise ship – there were no lido decks and outdoor pools, no central air-conditioning and (especially for the American cruise market) far too few cabins with private bathroom facilities. By 1967, her thirty-first year, the once highly successful *Queen Mary* showed a loss of £750,000 ($1.8 million). That summer, Cunard management had to face the harsh reality – both *Queens* had to be retired.

On that September morning in 1967, the *Queen Mary* departed from New York, finishing her Cunard trans-Atlantic career and all but ending a grand and glamorous era of ocean liner travel. She had a very impressive record: 1,000 crossings, carried 2,112,000 passengers and steamed 3,792,277 miles. Known to millions, there remained one oddity – she had never visited her home port of Liverpool.

In her final season, rumours circulated about the *Queen Mary*'s future – becoming a casino at Gibraltar, a migrant ship on the UK–Australia run or a high school moored along the Brooklyn waterfront in New York harbour or simply going to Japanese scrappers. In the end, the City of Long Beach in southern California bought her for $3,450,000 for use as a tourist attraction, museum, hotel and collection of shops and restaurants.

As the deal was signed, the *Queen Mary* set off from Southampton, on 31 October, with 1,040 nostalgic passengers on her farewell cruise. The thirty-nine-day voyage, the longest in her commercial days, took the world's last three-funnel liner to Lisbon, Las Palmas, Rio de Janeiro,

Valparaiso, Callao, Balboa, Acapulco and finally to Los Angeles. She flew a 310-foot-long (for 31 years) paying off pennant. Each of her 800 crew (reduced from 1,200) received a £40 farewell bonus.

After undergoing an exhaustive, three-year refit, costing $72 million and bringing her up to strict US Coast Guard safety standards, she finally opened, on 10 May 1971, as a tourist attraction. With varying degrees of success and fluctuating attendance figures and a series of operators, the *Queen Mary* has endured. The ship itself celebrated its seventy-fifth anniversary in 2001.

Long-retired Cunard crew members often visit the *Queen Mary*. Eammon Riley was a steward aboard the *Queen Mary* in 1957 and visited the ship at Long Beach over fifty years later. 'I am glad that she has been saved. She represents a bygone era, a lost grandeur and style,' he recalled. 'As I walked the decks, the corridors and into those grand lounges, I had tears in my eyes. The *Queen Mary* was a wonderful ship – and she gave us wonderful memories!'

Left: The *Queen Mary,* introduced in 1936, became one of the most successful, popular and heroic liners of all time. (Cunard)

Above: The hull of the 1,018-foot-long *Queen Mary* under construction at the John Brown shipyard in Clydebank, Scotland. (Cunard)

Above: Arriving at Southampton for the first time, the *Queen Mary* is heading to the King George V Graving Dock for final inspection. The *Majestic* and *Windsor Castle* are berthed on the right. (Cunard)

Left: Her Majesty Queen Mary (far right) names the *Queen Mary* during the launching ceremonies in September 1934. (Cunard)

Right: At 81,235 tons, the mighty *Queen Mary* is comparatively fitted into London's Trafalgar Square. (Cunard)

QUEEN MARY
PLAN of
TOURIST CLASS

DATE OF ISSUE
AUGUST 1937
REVISION OF
FEBRUARY 1937 ISSUE

FORM C 517
T T C. 92084

**BOOK THRU YOUR LOCAL AGENT
NO ONE CAN SERVE YOU BETTER**

CUNARD WHITE STAR LINE

25 BROADWAY
638 FIFTH AVENUE
NEW YORK CITY
OFFICES AND AGENCIES EVERYWHERE

Left: A Tourist Class deck plan aboard the new *Queen Mary.* (Norman Knebel Collection)

Far left: The towering *Queen Mary* in a night-time view in the King George V Graving Dock. (Author's Collection)

Opposite above: Crossing the Atlantic in 1938 aboard the *Queen Mary.* (Cunard)

Opposite below: The art deco splendour of the First Class main lounge aboard the 2,139-passenger *Queen Mary.* (Cunard)

Opposite right: Another deco gem: the First Class smoking room aboard the *Queen Mary.* (Cunard)

QUEEN ELIZABETH

QUEEN MARY

MAURETANIA

CARONIA

1st Class~

Left: First Class in the 1950s, when Cunard carried one-third of all Atlantic passengers. (Norman Knebel Collection)

Right: Jet aircraft began flying the Atlantic in October 1958 and quickly changed the role of the ocean liner. (Author's Collection)

Opposite above: The *Queen Mary* was one of the most popular ships – with passengers and crew alike – of all time. (Cunard)

Opposite below: During the war, with over 15,000 soldier-passengers aboard the *Queen Mary*, there were eight sessions of breakfast and eight sessions of dinner, 20 minutes each, and no lunch. (Cunard)

Opposite left: During her heroic wartime period, the *Queen Mary* established a record – 16,683 aboard during a voyage in July 1943. (Author's Collection)

19. MAURETANIA (1939)

For me, watching from the Hoboken shoreline and just across from the all-but-crowded steamship piers of New York City, Saturday mornings in the 1950s and early 1960s were special. Within an hour or so, beginning at 11 a.m., five or six liners would depart, sail past in a sort of procession, a convoy even, and head off on romantic voyages to faraway places. There were so many occasions and, as I recall, the 'second' *Mauretania* as we called her was often among them. She would have departed from either Pier 90 or 92, Cunard's berths, at 11.30. The procession might include an Italian liner such as the *Saturnia*, the *America*, the *Flandre*, the *New York* of the Greek Line and possibly the *Kungsholm*. Each ship was different. Each had a personality. But to me, the *Mauretania* had a special grace about her, a kind of ocean liner dignity. She was in every way a great liner, in ways an ultimate liner. In her design, I always thought, Cunard created one of the most perfect looking liners of all.

At the launching on 28 July 1938 of the second *Mauretania*, Lady Bates, the wife of the Cunard chairman, did the honours at the Cammell Laird & Company shipyard at Birkenhead, and remarked:

I count myself extremely fortunate in having been asked to launch this great ship. This is a red-letter day, not only for me but for Merseyside. The launch of the largest ship ever built in England, I hope that like her namesake, she may work her way into the affections of all who have anything to do with her on both sides of the Atlantic.

At 35,655 tons, the twin-funnel *Mauretania* was constructed between the *Queen Mary* in 1936 and the *Queen Elizabeth*, due out in the spring of 1940. She was to be something of a 'relief ship', substituting for one of the bigger, faster *Queens* during overhaul periods. The twin-screw *Mauretania* could make 23 knots, providing a six-day crossing, however. The *Queens*, which averaged 28½ knots, ran five-day passages. Often said to be a smaller version of the twin-funnel *Queen Elizabeth*, the *Mauretania* was smaller and often appraised as being 'more clubby, even more intimate' than the large, hotel-like *Queens*. Carrying as many as 1,140 passengers (470 First Class, 370 Cabin and 300 Tourist) and a crew of 593, the *Mauretania* also had a rather large cargo capacity, five holds in all, but which was never fully used. With a somewhat different appearance to either of the *Queens*, the *Mauretania* had a certain similarity to P&O's biggest liners of the day, the *Stratheden* and *Strathallan*. Alone, all three ships each had a set for forward kingposts.

The 772-foot-long *Mauretania* had barely entered commercial service, in June 1939 (first on a Liverpool–New York crossing, then on London–New York service), when war erupted in Europe. Nostalgically, four passengers onboard the maiden crossing had been aboard the first *Mauretania*'s maiden voyages over thirty years before, in 1907. The new liner was quickly painted in grey and her posted Cunard schedules disrupted. She was idle at New York for several months, over the winter of 1939/40, but then was officially called up for war duties on 6 March 1940. She sailed for the next six years as a heroic wartime trooper, carrying up to 9,000 troops per voyage.

On her first military voyage, she sailed via Panama to Sydney, where her luxury passenger fittings were removed and sent to storage. Her wartime exploits included a collision with a tanker outside New York harbour and an around-the-world voyage made in less than three months. By August 1946, she was released from war service, having carried 335,000 troops and, in forty-eight trooping voyages, sailed 540,000 miles.

After refitting, she was back in Cunard service – Southampton, Le Havre and Cobh to New York – in April 1947. She had a loyal following, but her predecessor, which held the Blue Riband for twenty-two years, always remained the more famous. Otherwise, the new *Mauretania*'s distinction of being the largest liner yet built in England (bigger British ships were constructed in either Scotland and Northern Ireland) was not surpassed until 1960, with advent of the *Windsor Castle* (also built at

Birkenhead) and the *Oriana* (created at Barrow-in-Furness).

Unlike the two *Queens*, the *Mauretania* went cruising in wintertime during the 1950s. Usually used for two- and three-week voyages to the Caribbean, she offered the occasional longer voyage – such as a trip to Peru in 1954.

Soon after the airlines secured greater numbers of passengers in 1959–63, the *Mauretania* was quick to fall on hard times. She sometimes crossed the Atlantic with as few as 300 passengers, a quarter of her capacity. Cunard managers looked to alternate operations, but not always with great success. In September 1962, during an overhaul, the *Mauretania* was, like some aging dowager, given a cosmetic makeover. She was repainted in 'cruising green', making for a more tropical, even leisurely, look. In the following March, she was assigned to a new Cunard Atlantic service – Naples, Genoa, Cannes and Gibraltar to New York. It was a highly misguided venture at best. Cunard lost millions. Virtually unknown to Mediterranean passengers, once again the *Mauretania* often carried as few as a third of her capacity. She had fierce competition from the well-known likes of the Italian and American Export lines, and much more modern competitors like the Italian Line's *Leonardo da Vinci*. The Cunarder was soon back in normal Cunard service, but limited to year-round cruising. In the end, there were charter voyages – carrying sales representatives of the Ford Motor Company and to carry guests to the opening of a new refinery in Wales (which included HM the Queen Mother coming aboard for lunch).

The Mauretania was decommissioned in November 1965 and, after being partially stripped, sailed for Inverkeithing to be scrapped.

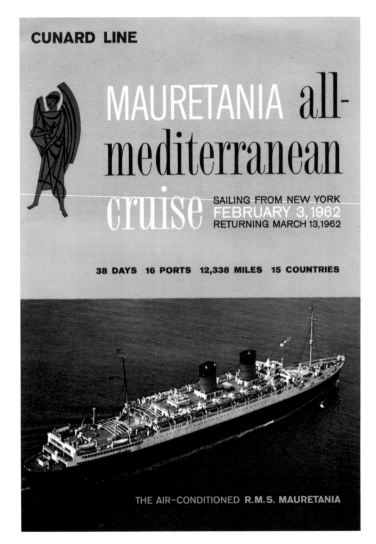

CUNARD LINE

MAURETANIA all-mediterranean cruise

SAILING FROM NEW YORK
FEBRUARY 3, 1962
RETURNING MARCH 13, 1962

38 DAYS 16 PORTS 12,338 MILES 15 COUNTRIES

THE AIR-CONDITIONED R.M.S. MAURETANIA

Above: In her final years, 1963–65, the *Mauretania* was repainted in Cunard's so-called 'cruising green'. She is seen here outbound in New York's Lower Bay. (Author's Collection)

Right: On 5 October 1953, the 772-foot-long *Mauretania* docked herself during a New York harbour tugboat strike. With 1,024 passengers aboard, she was only 25 minutes late. (Cronican-Arroyo Collection)

Opposite above: Outbound after an afternoon sailing at New York. (Cunard)

Opposite below: With the war over, the *Mauretania* returns Canadian soldiers to Halifax in this view from the summer of 1945. (Halifax Maritime Museum)

Opposite left: A long cruise to the Mediterranean for the *Mauretania* in the winter of 1962. (Cunard)

20. QUEEN ELIZABETH (1940)

In the mid-1960s, the great Cunard *Queens* kept up their high season tandem crossings. They would layover in New York usually on Tuesday evenings. Pier security was friendly and lenient and, being keen ship enthusiasts, would allow us aboard. We would visit them, the *Queens*. The day's work was over, the inbound passengers long disembarked and the crew gone ashore, mostly for a night on the town. Well lighted but empty, those big liners were like big tombs. With their bucket lamps, polished woods and glossy lino floors, they did represent a bygone era. Modern ships such as the *France* and *Michelangelo* had appeared and turned the *Queens* into frumpy versions of a bygone age. We had yet to appreciate their art deco-style, 1930s interiors and features. But how fortunate we were – exploring the great *Queen Mary* and *Queen Elizabeth*! Little did we realise that their days were numbered.

Cunard's brilliant scheme to have a two-ship trans-Atlantic service with a weekly sailing in each direction produced the most famous of liners ever built. The *Queen Mary* came first and because of this and her record breaking speed, she was always the slightly more famous and the more preferred by passengers as well as crew. 'The *Queen Mary* had a certain high style, a grandeur, that the *Queen Elizabeth* did not,' according to Adam Woods, a Cunard crewmember in the 1960s. 'The *Queen Mary* was pre-war, the *Elizabeth* was more post-war. Even the tone and mood aboard each ship was different. You could feel it – and almost immediately.'

The *Queen Elizabeth* was also the last of the ships covered as Cunard-White Star liners of the 1930s. The *Mary* came into service in the 1930s, the great age of the superliner, along with the likes of the *Bremen*, *Rex* and *Normandie*. The new Cunarder had a spectacular maiden voyage that received worldwide press. Almost immediately, she had a great reputation. Alternately, the second of the *Queens* – while designed and constructed in the thirties – did not experience this initial glamour and notoriety. In fact, she arrived without a gala maiden crossing, but instead arrived quietly, painted in grey and without a welcoming armada of escorting tugs and spraying fireboats. The *Elizabeth* had to wait – she was pressed almost immediately into war service.

The secrecy that surrounded the naming of the *Queen Mary* was not true for this second Cunard giant. The name *Queen Elizabeth* was known from the start. Her first keel plate was laid on 4 December 1936 at the John Brown yard on the Clyde. It had also been decided from the beginning that the two liners would be quite different. The *Elizabeth* would be more contemporary, even more modern, with two instead of three funnels, less cluttering on her upper, outer decks and with more of a rake to her bow. The new liner would show improvements down below as well – with twelve boilers instead of the *Queen Mary*'s twenty-four. Cunard had also learned much from the very innovative *Normandie*. Cunard engineers, disguised as passengers and staff, crossed on the French flagship and took copious notes.

The construction of the 1,031-foot-long *Queen Elizabeth* – the world's longest liner – was given high priority. Shipyard crews at Clydebank worked round the clock, aided by huge floodlights attached to the cranes and building slips for night as well as dark winter shifts. On 27 September 1938, the huge hull – then weighing in at 40,000 tons – was named by HM Queen Elizabeth, who was accompanied by Princess Elizabeth and Princess Margaret. Actually, the ship itself began to move along the slipways and into the River Clyde before the Queen had begun her speech. Fortunately, she was quick to release the bottle of wine and to name the ship.

During the following year, and as the political situation in Europe became increasingly more serious, finishing the *Elizabeth* was no longer a high priority. Many of the shipyard's work crews were assigned to more urgently needed warships. The liner's interiors were left unfinished, often in shell-like conditions. Only essential plumbing and electrical work were completed. In London, a proposal was made that the still incomplete ship should be sold to the neutral United States. After all, so some thought, the big liner would be nothing more than a big target to Nazi attackers.

The *Queen Elizabeth* became an increasingly greater worry. There were rumours that Nazi bombers were planning to bomb the Clyde, the shipyards and in particular the new Cunarder. It would be a great blow to British morale to finish-off the brand-new *Elizabeth*. On 6 February 1940 (her commercial maiden crossing was to have started on 24 April), Winston Churchill – then First Lord of Admiralty – ordered the ship away from British shores. Halifax was considered, but New York was the final choice and where she would join, in safe moorings, the *Queen Mary*. It was all top-secret at the time. Some false news was spread, however. Mostly, this was the plan to first send the *Elizabeth* to Southampton, for final dry docking and outfitting, before steaming off to America. This scheme to mislead the Luftwaffe obviously worked. On the same day that the ship was due to arrive in Southampton, enemy bombers were found to be circling over the English Channel. Clearly, they were waiting for the liner. Fortunately, and with a handful of shipyard workers and even the Clyde pilot still aboard, the *Elizabeth* sped at high speed across the Irish Sea, past Northern Ireland and then across the Atlantic. The Nazis were furious. She reached the safety of New York harbour on 7 March and was promptly dubbed the 'grey ghost'.

Together with the *Queen Mary* and *Normandie*, the *Queen Elizabeth* remained at Pier 90 for eight months. During that time, only completion to her passenger spaces could be done. Any military work would have violated America's neutral status at the time. She followed the *Queen Mary* by going out East, but to Singapore instead of Sydney for further dry docking. The early war years featured many rumours. One was that the 83,673 grt *Queen Elizabeth* – the world's largest liner as well – might be converted to a huge aircraft carrier. The same rumours were applied to the idle *Normandie*, which remained at New York. Gutting the *Elizabeth*'s otherwise brand-new inner decks meant she could be used to store as many as 270 aircraft. Alternately, another rumour suggested a plan of combination troopship-aircraft carrier – with up to 6,000 troops and forty-eight aircraft.

The quadruple-screw *Elizabeth* was first assigned to Indian Ocean troop service, sailing between Sydney and Port Suez in Egypt. She was teamed with the *Queen Mary* as well as such other trooper-liners like the *Aquitania, Nieuw Amsterdam, Mauretania* and *Empress of Britain*. Passenger loads were quite impressive for the time – in the spring of 1941, the *Queen Elizabeth* left Sydney with 5,600 troops onboard while the *Queen Mary* departed with 6,000 and the *Mauretania* with 4,400.

Both *Queens* were moved back onto the North Atlantic in 1942 and refitted to carry as many as 15,000 troops per weekly crossing. Both liners became the greatest troopships of all time. It was all far from the luxuries that Cunard had planned. The troops slept in tiered 'standee' bunks that were actually stretcher-like contraptions made of canvas slung between steel poles. They required a minimum of space and stood as much as six high. Consequently, a two-berth cabin in First Class could now sleep as many as twenty. These standee berths were also placed in the public rooms, leaving only two dining rooms and two lounges. For dining, there were eight twenty-minute sessions of breakfast and eight sessions of dinner each day; there was no lunch in wartime.

The *Queens* – dubbed 'the biggins' by soldiers and crews – were given high priority during the war years. They were meticulously guarded. Even at New York, however, saboteurs managed to get aboard and plug some fire hoses, drill holes in several lifeboats and, in April 1943, two bombs were found aboard the *Queen Elizabeth*.

In all, the *Queens* gave impeccable service during the war and survived unharmed and intact. The *Elizabeth* was selected to be a symbol of British peace and post-war prosperity and so was refitted first. After delivering her last load of troops (on westbound voyages by then, of course), she returned to Southampton on 16 June 1946. She was later sent to the Clyde for a full restoration. As her military fittings were removed, furniture and other items were removed from storage. In the end, everything had to be gathered in a huge warehouse for sorting and assignment onboard. Work went on around the clock. Altogether, there were 21,000 pieces of furniture

and these included 4,500 sofas, chairs and tables. Along with 2,000 carpets, there were 6,000 pairs of curtains and bedspreads. The *Queen Elizabeth* – carrying 823 in First Class, 662 in Cabin Class and 798 in Tourist Class – finally left Southampton on her commercial maiden voyage to New York on 16 October 1946. Although over six years old, the liner finally had her traditional maiden arrival reception of tugs, fireboats and spectator boats. She was joined by the *Queen Mary* in the following summer and so finally Cunard's two-ship express service was in operation.

The *Queens* were the most spectacular pair of liners ever built and headed the great Cunard fleet. The *Elizabeth* was flagship, commanded by the company's commodore. 'Getting there was half the fun' was Cunard's marketing slogan and, at its peak, in the mid-1950s, the line carried one-third of all Atlantic passengers. In 1958, Cunard was its peak with no less than twelve liners in regular service to the United States and Canada: *Queen Elizabeth, Queen Mary, Mauretania, Caronia, Britannic, Saxonia, Ivernia, Carinthia, Sylvania, Media, Parthia* and *Scythia*.

Like almost all Atlantic liners, the *Queens* lost more and more passengers to the airlines by the early 1960s – and soon lost more and more money. While Cunard was planning to retire the *Queen Mary* (by September 1967), Cunard directors decided to keep the *Queen Elizabeth* (until as late as 1975) as a companion to the new *Queen* then being built on the Clyde. In the winter of 1965/66, the *Elizabeth* was specially given an extensive refit and modernisation. Complete air-conditioning, a swimming pool and lido, and far more private cabin flooding were added. It was expected that the ship could also do more lucrative cruising as well. Instead, the *Queen* continued to make staggering losses. When it was decided to retire the *Queen Mary* in September 1967, the *Elizabeth* would now follow as well, but in October 1968.

Following somewhat in the *Queen Mary*'s path, the *Queen Elizabeth* – by then relisted as being 82,998 gross tons – was sent to America for use as a hotel, tourist attraction, museum and collection of shops and restaurants. While Philadelphia was the first consideration, Port Everglades, Florida, was the ultimate choice. So confident in the venture was Cunard that it retained an 85 per cent share in the project. But after two years berthed in the harsh Florida sun, little occurred. There were big financial problems, neglect and disinterest and the once mighty *Elizabeth* began to deteriorate. Finally, she went to the auction block and, in September 1970, found a new owner in Taiwanese shipping magnate C. Y. Tung. His plan was to bring the ship to Hong Kong, refit her as the world's first floating university-cruise ship and to roam the world on varied itineraries. She was renamed *Seawise University* ('Seawise' being a variation on the owner's initials: C. Y.). Registered in the Bahamas, the initial voyage out to the Far East hinted of further trouble for the once impeccable Cunard flagship. The voyage was long, complicated by mechanical breakdowns and a two-month wait being anchored off Aruba for repairs.

The new career of the former *Queen Elizabeth* was not to be. After undergoing $6 million in refitting at a Hong Kong anchorage, the liner was being readied for final dry docking in Japan in the winter of 1972. Fires suspiciously broke out and spread rapidly through the anchored ship on 9 January. Fireboats rushed to the scene and poured tons of water on the blazing ship. On the following morning, the severely damaged *Seawise University* turned on her side and capsized. She was ruined, a total loss.

Talks of salvage and possible repairs and rebuilding were short-lived. In the end, the only future was in scrapping. Her remains were hauled away. Her record was one of the greatest of all Atlantic liners. And assuredly, the *Queen Elizabeth* was one of the great ships that belonged to this group, belonged in this book – the Cunard-White Star Liners of the 1930s.

The mighty *Queen Elizabeth*, heavily loaded with returning troops, is seen arriving in New York in the summer of 1945. (Author's Collection)

QUEEN MARY AND QUEEN ELIZABETH FROM THE AIR.   C.M.500A

Above: Outbound from New York, the *Queen Elizabeth* makes a late morning departure from Luxury Liner Row. (Cunard)

Below: The *Queens* meet at Southampton in October 1946 – the newly refitted *Queen Elizabeth* is on the left; the *Queen Mary*, still in war dress, arrives on the right. (Cunard)

Right: The 1,031-foot-long *Queen Elizabeth* – the world's largest liner – takes a turn in the King George V Graving Dock at Southampton.

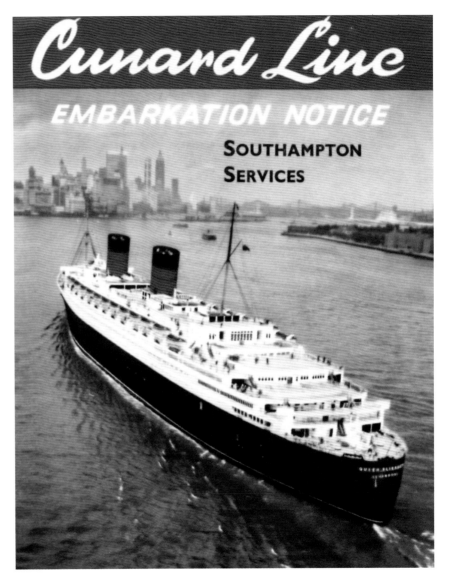

Above: A tag for stateroom baggage aboard Cunard in the 1950s and 1960s. (Author's Collection)

Right: Embarkation notices for 1962. (Andrew Kilk Collection)

Left: Tourist-class fares for five nights to Southampton from New York began at $175 in the early 1960s. (Andrew Kilk Collection)

Right: Lasting link: the *Queen Mary* in her retirement at Long Beach, California. (Hotel Queen Mary)

Above: The *Queen Elizabeth* at Southampton's Ocean Terminal in the 1960s. The liners *Northern Star* (left) and *Argentina* are at the top. (Cunard)

Right: A menu cover for a commemorative dinner celebrating the fiftieth anniversary of the launch of the *Queen Elizabeth.* (Author's Collection)

1938

50TH ANNIVERSARY - RMS QUEEN ELIZABETH

RMS QUEEN ELIZABETH 1938, 83,673 TONS

QUEEN ELIZABETH 2 1988, 67,140 TONS

1988

BIBLIOGRAPHY

Braynard, Frank O. and William H. Miller, *Fifty Famous Liners* (Cambridge, England: Patrick Stephens Ltd, 1982).

De Kerbrech, Richard P. and David L. Williams, *Cunard White Star Liners of the 1930s* (London, England: Conway Maritime Press Ltd, 1988).

Haws, Duncan, *Merchant Fleets: Cunard Line* (Hereford, England: TCL Publications, 1987).

Haws, Duncan, *Merchant Fleets: White Star Line* (Hereford, England: TCL Publications, 1990).

Le Fleming, H. M., *Cunard White Star Liners of the 1930s* (London, England: Ian Allan Ltd, 1960).

Miller, William H., *Under the Red Ensign: British Passenger Liners of the '50s & '60s* (Stroud, Gloucestershire, UK, 2009).

Miller, William H., *The Last Atlantic Liners* (London: Conway Maritime Press Ltd, 1985).

Miller, William H., *The Last Blue Water Liners* (London: Conway Maritime Press Ltd, 1986).

Newall, Peter, *Cunard Line: A Fleet History* (Longton, Preston, UK: Ships in Focus Publications, 2013).